Café Cakes
By Tim Fisher
© 2020

Contents

Foreword

When someone claims to make the best brownie in the world – and especially when that someone also happens to be an award-winning pastry chef – it becomes my highest priority to taste this brownie. So, on a sunny day I caught the train to Croydon to Tim's little chocolate shop and spent what might have been hours chatting to him across the glass display cabinet. This man knew his chocolate. If I'm honest, I can't remember the brownie well, but I do remember his lemon chocolate. I know the brownie must have been good, it's just that I have eaten many, many brownies since then. I also had the good fortune of spending an afternoon with Tim and two friends as he taught us how to make the most incredible layered chocolate dessert. That one I do still dream of.

Alongside his generosity, what sets Tim apart, I think, is his absolute dedication to perfection. He told us stories that day in his kitchen of his training, where he made many variations of a recipe where just one variable was changed at a time in order to fully understand the effect of too much or too little of every ingredient. I suspect he's the kind of chef who would not just know whether a recipe would work, just by looking at it, but also exactly how it would taste. You are sure to be in safe hands with any of his recipe books and I am honoured to write the introduction to this one.

Jennifer Earle

About Tim

Award winning pastry chef Tim Fisher has over 30 years experience as a pastry chef, baker & chocolatier. In his career Tim has won over 50 competition awards, these include: Winner of the dessert of the year competition in 2004, over 30 medals at the British Open Cookery Championships including; 13 best in class and the category winner's plate for the best pastry entry in the 2016 competition. Tim holds a diploma in advanced culinary arts from Thames Valley University and has also studied at the national bakery schools in both London and Switzerland.

Tim worked for many years in London running pastry sections at numerous sites including The London Capital Club, BBC TV centre at White City, London Business School and many prestigious law firms and banks in the city of London. After many years of working long hours and commuting to London Tim decided to use his pastry skills to teach and now runs his highly successful pastry classes in Surrey teaching his skills to "professionals and keen amateurs alike".

Please go to page 95 for more details about Tim's pastry classes.

Tim is keen to pass on his experience and knowledge to help people make fabulous dishes at home, these recipes are his personal creations developed during his 30 years working with some great chefs, particularly the brilliant and inspirational Professor John Huber.

Café Cakes is Tim's third book following the publication of Biscuits & Cookies in 2018 and Tarts & Pies in 2019.

Before You Start

Baking cakes is basically a science, whilst decorating them to present to your loved ones is possibly art. I think far greater emphasis should be placed onto the quality of the flavour and texture of a cake than to how it looks, but it's nice when you can get all of the aspects right. Hopefully by following the guidance in this book you will achieve all of these goals. I have spent over 30 years developing recipes that really work and that I hope you will find quite easy to follow. It's one thing to be able to make a perfect cake it's quite another to convey this on paper so that others can do it too. I have been teaching pastry, baking and chocolate classes as Tim's Pastry Club for the last 5 years as well as to junior chefs working under me in the jobs I have held before that in the last 25 years.

Many of my personal methods and working practises are nonconformist and to some quite odd. What usually happens in my classes is that people say things like "Oh what I usually do it this" or "so and so in their book does it like that". By the end of the class I normally get "wow that's the best cake I have ever made or "I never would have thought to do it like that". I teach people how the ingredients react to each other in certain conditions and to understand how to get the best out of their baking.

In the back part of this book there are sections on cake making methods, storage, equipment and ingredients and where to purchase these from. I urge you to read these before you start as the information contained there is vital to obtaining great results. What I would say right up front is purchase some airtight containers, not plastic tubs with ill fitting lids but proper airtight containers. I use the ones made by Stewarts which I purchase through Nisbets, I could not work without them.

Each dish has been thoroughly tested to bake at the temperature stated in the recipe taking into account the density of the batter, levels of sugar and moisture and the ideal tin to bake the cake in.

Before you start I would advise you to read the recipes carefully, check you have the correct equipment and ingredients, weigh your recipes precisely, preheat your oven and follow the instructions carefully and you should get great results.

Happy Baking!

American Coffee Cake

Makes 16 pieces

Crumble Topping
60g plain flour
140g light brown sugar
3 tsp ground cinnamon
60g unsalted butter (cool and cut into small chunks)
pinch of salt
Cake
200g plain flour
½ tsp baking powder
¼ tsp bicarbonate of soda
pinch of salt
90g softened unsalted butter
115g caster sugar
2 tsp vanilla extract
1 medium egg
1 medium egg yolk
150g sour cream

1. Preheat the oven to 160°C (non fan oven 180°C).
2. Line a 24cm square cake tin with parchment paper and place aside.
3. For the crumble weigh the flour, sugar, cinnamon and salt in the bowl for a stand mixer.
4. Add the 60g of butter and mix slowly until a nice gritty crumble is formed.
5. Remove the crumble mix and tip into a bowl then place aside.
6. Weigh the flour, baking powder, salt and bicarbonate of soda in a bowl.
7. Sift onto a separate piece of parchment and place aside.
8. Make the cake in the same machine bowl you used for the crumble.
9. Place the 90g of butter, caster sugar and vanilla into the bowl.
10. Cream using the whisk attachment on medium speed for 4-5 minutes.
11. Add the egg yolk and whisk in until smooth then add the whole egg.
12. Whisk in until smooth then remove the bowl from the machine.
13. Add half of the sifted dry ingredients and fold in gently with a marls.
14. Add all of the sour cream in one go and mix in until smooth.
15. Add the remaining dry ingredients and fold in until smooth and lump free.
16. Scrape into the lined cake tin and spread level.
17. Sprinkle the crumble topping evenly over the cake.
18. Bake for 35-40 minutes or until the centre is springy and a skewer comes out clean.
19. Leave to cool in the tin for 30 minutes then lift still on the paper into an airtight box.
20. To serve remove the edges then cut the cake into 16 even pieces (4 x 4).

American Coffee Cake is a paradox in that it's not coffee flavoured but is in fact a cake you would ideally consume with a cup of coffee hence the name. The cake is very simple to make and similar to a typical British traybake. The recipe contains sour cream which gives a lovely texture and slight acidic bite to the cake which contrasts beautifully with the crunchy sweet cinnamon topping.

I add quite a hit of vanilla which gives the cake a lovely perfume. Unusually there is a yolk and a whole egg which results in a more tender cake crumb. The crumble topping is heavily flavoured with cinnamon which bakes into a lovely crunchy fragrant topping. You could swap the spice in the crumble topping for cardamom or ginger both of which are delicious. This is not a common cake in the UK but do give it a try it's delicious!

Tim's Tips

- Sour cream is easy to get hold of, don't use ordinary cream it won't work the same.
- Sprinkle the crumble mix over the cake with your fingers to break it up.
- Bake until the sponge springs back, do not overbake it as it dries out quickly.
- Needless to say the perfect accompaniment is fresh coffee.
- Be careful when checking the baked cake as the crumble topping is very hot.

Apple Cake

Makes one 20cm cake

Apples
30g unsalted butter + 30g caster sugar
6 pink lady apples (450g net weight of apple)
Cake
90g unsalted butter
100g caster sugar
few drops apple flavour (optional)
2 medium eggs
150g plain flour
1½ tsp baking powder
80g whipping cream
Topping
1 tsp ground cinnamon
30g demerara sugar

1. Preheat the oven to 170°C (non fan oven 190°C).
2. Line a 20cm spring form tin with parchment paper and place aside.
3. Line a small tray with parchment paper and place into the freezer or fridge.
4. Weigh the flour and baking powder in a bowl.
5. Sift the dry ingredients onto a separate piece of parchment and place aside.
6. Peel the apples, quarter and remove the cores then cut each quarter into 4 pieces.
7. Cook the apples in the 30g of butter and 30g of sugar over a high heat.
8. When nicely cooked place onto the pre-chilled tray and place back into the freezer.
9. Place the butter, flavour (if using) and sugar into the bowl for a stand mixer.
10. Cream with the whisk attachment on medium speed for 3-4 minutes.
11. Add the eggs one at a time beating each in well then scrape the bowl down.
12. Add half of the sifted dry ingredients to the bowl and fold in with a maris.
13. Add half of the cream to the bowl and fold in carefully.
14. Add the remaining sifted dry ingredients and fold in gently.
15. Add the remaining cream and half of the cooked apples to the bowl.
16. Fold in slowly until smooth and completley blended.
17. Scrape the batter into the tin and spread level with the back of a spoon.
18. Place the remaining apples evenly on the top of the batter.
19. Sprinkle the cake with the cinnamon and then the demerara sugar.
20. Bake for 45-50 minutes until springy and a skewer comes out clean.
21. Leave to cool in the tin for 20 minutes.
22. Remove the cake from the tin and place into an airtight container.

Pink Lady Apples are my favourite variety of apple to use for desserts and baking. They make the best Tarte Tatin as they keep their shape whilst cooking retaining their delicious flavour. These characteristics also make Pink Lady apples perfect for this cake as they are cooked first then added to the batter. This cake has two unusual features, firstly a little cream is added to the batter which gives it a lovely richness and secondly a little apple flavour in preference to vanilla. The apple flavouring is optional but I love the aroma it imparts to the cake over the much used vanilla.

The trick with the apples is to cook them so they are slightly coloured but with a little firmness so that they do not disintegrate during baking. Adding the dry ingredients and cream alternately makes the cake less tough during the mixing and helps keeps the cake tender.

Tim's Tips

- **Pink Lady apples are superb, if you can't get them Braeburn are a good swap.**
- **Don't stir the apples when cooking, shake the pan and keep them moving.**
- **Use a large pan that is very hot or the apples will boil rather than colour.**
- **Make sure the cooked apples are cold before adding to the batter.**
- **If you like a lot of cinnamon in your cakes you can add more.**
- **Don't take the cake out of the tin too early or it may collapse.**
- **I tend to leave the cake on the base of the tin until cold then gently remove.**
- **A slice of the cake gently warmed makes an excellent dessert served with whipped cream or ice cream and caramel sauce.**

Banana Loaf Cake

Makes one loaf cake

90g unsalted butter (slightly softened)
115g caster sugar
few drops banana flavour (optional)
2 medium eggs
180g plain flour
2 tsp baking powder
240g very ripe banana (net weight)
1 tsp whole milk
20g demerara sugar

1. Preheat the oven to 160°C (non fan oven 180°C).
2. Line a 1lb loaf tin with parchment paper or a cake liner and place aside.
3. Weigh the flour and baking powder together in a bowl.
4. Sift onto a separate piece of parchment and place aside.
5. Place the butter and sugar into the bowl for a stand mixer.
6. If you are using the flavour add this to the bowl now.
7. Cream with the whisk attachment for 4-5 minutes until light.
8. Add the eggs one at time and beat each in well.
9. Remove the bowl from the machine and scrape down.
10. Add the dry ingredients and fold in carefully with a maris.
11. Mash the bananas in a bowl then add the milk to the bananas.
12. Add the banana and milk to the machine bowl.
13. Fold together carefully with a maris until smooth.
14. Place into the tin and spread level with the back of a spoon.
15. Sprinkle the demerara sugar evenly over the top of the cake.
16. Bake for 50-55 minutes or until a skewer comes out clean.
17. Leave to cool for 30 minutes in the tin.
18. Lift the cake out of the tin with the paper and place into an airtight container.

Banana Cake or bread (called this because it's baked in a loaf tin) is a dish in every baker's repertoire and everyone thinks theirs is the best. I tried many versions some made with butter some made with oil and different varieties of sugar. I also experimented with different blends of raising agents using both baking powder and bicarbonate of soda. In the end I decided to use unsalted butter in preference to oil as I prefer the richness it gives the texture of the finished cake. I eventually settled on just baking powder as I find the bicarbonate of soda darkened the cake crumb too much. I prefer the clean neutral flavour the caster sugar gives the cake allowing the banana flavour to really come through.

After all my experimenting I ended up with this recipe which on balance I think is pretty good. I used extremely ripe bananas to get the depth of flavour I was looking for. The banana flavouring should only be used if your bananas aren't extremely ripe and as a last resort. As with all cakes that contain fruit the texture is heavier than a normal cake but this version is relatively light with a good punchy banana flavour. I tried several batches to see how much banana puree I could get into the cake and found that 240g was the maximum, any more than that left a wet seam at the base of the cake.

Tim's Tips

- **Use the very ripest bananas possible.**

- **I only use the flavour if the bananas are not as ripe as I would like.**

- **The milk helps keep the cake moist, semi-skimmed milk is fine.**

- **I prefer to mash the bananas to a rough puree but make sure there are no large lumps of banana, a potato masher is perfect for this job.**

- **Don't mash the bananas until you have made the batter or they go brown, add to the cake batter immediately after mashing with the milk.**

- **If you have more bananas than you need, immediately freeze them in the skins, then defrost as required. The flesh will be brown making the cake crumb a bit darker but the flavour will still be excellent.**

Battenberg

Makes 2 Battenberg cakes

1 tsp vanilla extract
1 tsp almond extract
180g unsalted butter (softened)
250g plain flour
1¼ tsp baking powder
1 tsp glycerine
5 medium eggs
265g caster sugar
red food colouring
yellow food colouring
100g prepared apricot jam (page 74)
225g marzipan for each cake (page 73)

1. Preheat the oven to 170°C (non fan oven 190°C).
2. If making your own marzipan make first as per the instructions on page 73.
3. Take a piece of card and make a strip the same height and width as the tin (this is for the divider in the centre of the tin).
4. Cut a piece of parchment the same width as the tin and 45cm in length.
5. Grease a 30cm x 20cm brownie tin with butter or spray grease.
6. Grease the card strip and place in the tin in the centre from side to side.
7. Cover with the parchment and press over the divider.
8. Press the parchment paper to the tin making sure the tin is equally divided in two.
9. Sift the flour and baking powder into the bowl for a stand mixer.
10. Add the butter to the bowl and mix slowly using the beater attachment for 1 minute.
11. When a paste forms stop the machine then add the glycerine and the flavours.
12. Beat on medium speed for 5-6 minutes until light.
13. Weigh the sugar in a bowl and leave to one side.
14. Place the eggs into a clean medium sized bowl.
15. Using a hand held electric mixer whisk the eggs on high speed.
16. Gradually add all the sugar and whisk for 2-3 minutes until pale and well risen.
17. Scrape a quarter of the eggs and sugar into the bowl with the flour and butter.
18. Beat in briefly until smooth on medium speed.
19. Add the remaining eggs and sugar in 3 additions on medium speed.
20. When adding the last batch of sugar and egg scrape the bowl down well.
21. Mix the batter briefly on medium speed until smooth.
22. Remove from the machine and mix gently with a maris to ensure it's smooth.
23. Weigh 460g of mixture into two separate bowls.
24. Colour one bowl pink and one bowl yellow making nice pastel shades.

25. Place each batter into the separate halves of the tin and spread level.*
    * I spread my mixture slightly thicker at the ends away from the divide.
26. Bake for 25-30 minutes until the sponges spring back.
27. Leave to cool in the tins for 5 minutes covered with a clean tea towel.
28. Remove the tea towel and place a sheet of parchment on top of the tin.
29. Place a baking sheet on top of the parchment and flip the tray over.
30. Leave the tin covering the cake and place aside to cool on the tray for 20 minutes.
31. Remove the tin and lift the cake still on the paper into an airtight container.
32. When completely cool turn the sponges over onto parchment paper.
33. Remove the top and bottom crusts by gently rubbing the crusts with your hand.
34. Trim the edges off the sponges and level them if necessary.
35. Place the two sponges onto the table and spread one with the apricot jam.
36. Place the other sponge on top press lightly and make sure they are level.
37. Measure and cut a block from the sponge 18cm long by 12cm wide.
38. Cut lengthways down the centre to obtain two strips 18cm x 6cm.
39. Cut each of these down the centre to obtain four strips 18cm x 3cm.
40. Place all four pieces on the table and brush two of them with apricot jam.
41. Place the other two sponges on top reversed to obtain the classic pattern.
42. If you are going to keep one or both cakes wrap in cling film and freeze.
43. Knead the marzipan briefly on the table to make pliable.
44. Roll the marzipan out using icing sugar shaken through a sieve.
45. Roll the marzipan into a rectangle 30cm x 20cm x 3mm thick.
46. Cut the marzipan to the length of the cake to ensure the correct size.
47. Cut the end straight then roll up the cake to measure the length of marzipan required to cover all 4 sides of the cake with a tiny overhang.
48. Cut the end straight, the rectangle should now fit the cake perfectly.
49. Unwrap the cake carefully from the marzipan and place the cake to one side.
50. Spread the rectangle of marzipan with a thin layer of the prepared apricot jam.
51. Place the cake on the edge of the marzipan and roll up carefully pressing lightly.
52. Press the cake gently on each side into the table as you roll to even the shape.
53. On the last turn there should be a very slight overlap press together to seal.
54. You can leave the edge plain or if you prefer crimp with tweezers or your fingers.
55. Leave the cake on a parchment lined tray for 1 hour to dry out slightly.
56. Cut the ends off to neaten the cake then cut into 8 slices.

Battenberg Cake was created to celebrate the wedding of Queen Victoria's granddaughter to Prince Louis of Battenberg in 1884. This cake was my number one favourite when I was kid. I used to plead with my mum to buy this for tea on a Sunday which she often did. I always loved the almond flavour hit and the pink and yellow light sponge, simple but gorgeous. This is another example of the flour batter method which is essential to obtain a firm textured but light sponge which is required to prevent the jam soaking into the cake.

The mixture produces enough batter to fill a 30cm x 20cm brownie tin which yields two Battenberg cakes so a bit of effort but a good return for your labours. The cakes without the marzipan freeze really well. I normally cover one with marzipan and freeze the other one. Commercially bought marzipan is quite soft and gets softer if you store it in an airtight box so I make my own which is firmer (page 73). After assembling I leave for an hour to dry out the marzipan a little then I cut the ends off to neaten.

Making an excellent Battenberg cake requires some skill and attention to detail so I have included pictures of how to put it together. Take your time and don't stress too much about getting it perfect as it takes practise. If you cut the cake to the dimensions I have stated here you should end up with two neat Battenberg cakes.

Tim's Tips

- Turning the cake onto a paper lined tray not only flattens the top but makes the crust soft enabling you to remove it easily with your hand.

- The neatness of the cake depends entirely on cutting the layers accurately. I use a ruler to measure and to help cut straight lines.

- Glycerine is a humectant and helps to extend the shelf life. It is quite easy to find in the supermarket but if you cannot get it just leave it out it's fine.

- Keep the marzipan in a plastic bag to avoid drying out. I use a disposable piping bag tied with cling film as the plastic is thick so this works really well.

- Adjust your almond extract depending on the strength. Use caution, you are looking for a delicate flavour.

- I colour my sponges by adding a drop of colour at a time until I get the shade I want. This depends entirely on the strength of the colouring so be cautious!

- The trimmings of pink and yellow sponge make fantastic trifle sponge. I use mine to make almond amaretto trifles which are delicious!

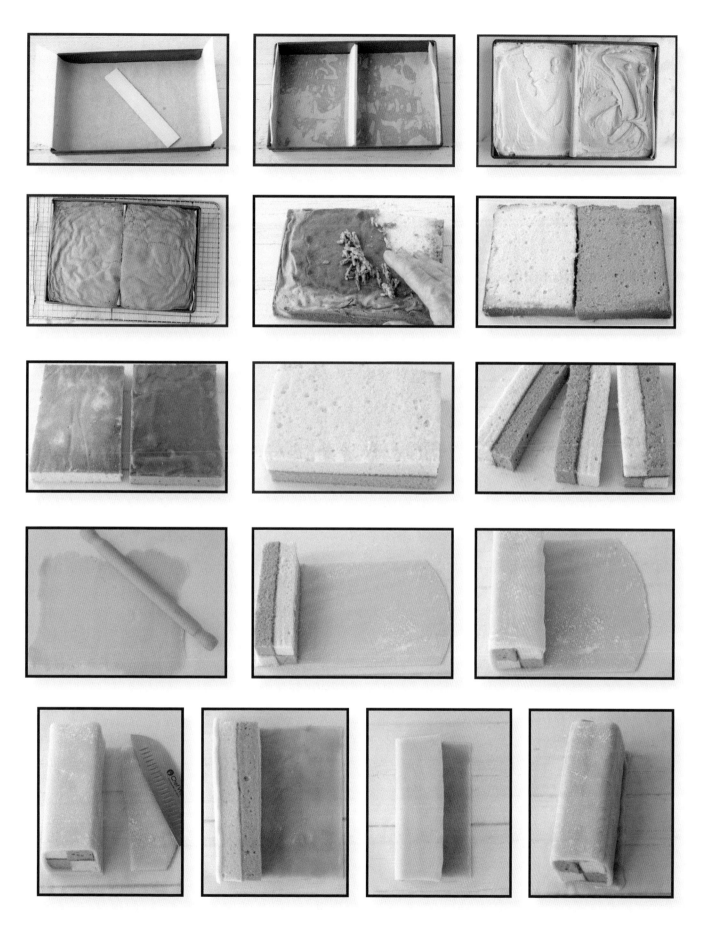

Blueberry & Almond Cake

15 Pieces of cake

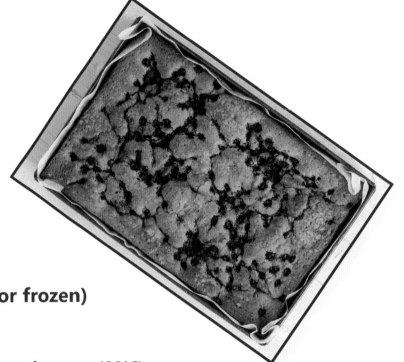

200g unsalted butter
200g caster sugar
½ tsp almond extract
4 medium eggs
125g plain flour
1 tsp baking powder
125g ground almonds
200g blueberries (fresh or frozen)
35g demerara sugar

1. Preheat the oven to 170°C (non fan oven 190°C).
2. Line a 30cm x 20cm brownie tin with parchment paper and place aside.
3. Weigh the flour and baking powder into a bowl.
4. Sift the dry ingredients onto a separate piece of parchment.
5. Weigh the ground almonds and place on top the sifted ingredients then place aside.
6. Place the butter, sugar and extract into a bowl for a stand mixer.
7. Using the whisk attachment cream for 3-4 minutes on medium speed.
8. Add the eggs one at a time mixing in each well on medium speed.
9. Remove the bowl from the machine and scrape down well.
10. Add the dry ingredients and fold together with a maris until smooth.
11. Scrape the mixture into the tin then spread level.
12. Scatter the blueberries evenly over the cake starting from the outside.
13. If the blueberries are frozen allow to defrost on the cake for 15 minutes.
14. Sprinkle the demerara sugar evenly over the cake.
15. Bake for 30-35 minutes.
16. When the cake is springy and a skewer comes out clean remove from the oven.
17. Place aside to cool for 30 minutes then lift the cake out with the paper.
18. Place into an airtight box until the next day.
19. To serve trim off the edges and cut the cake into 15 pieces (5 x 3).

Blueberries & almonds are a wonderful combination which I first saw paired together when Pierre Koffmann published a recipe for a blueberry financier. I wanted to combine these two flavours in a recipe of my own so I developed this traybake. The cake has a high ratio of almonds so remains lovely and moist with a slight gritty texture to the cake which marries beautifully with the blueberries. I have found that frozen blueberries actually work better than fresh because the frozen variety are picked when they are perfect so have a consistency of flavour and they are available all year round.

The benefit also of a tray bake is that the cake bakes fairly quickly so it doesn't dry out or have long enough in the oven to develop a thick crust. I like to cut the edges off to make the pieces even so that each person gets the same portion but the edges are delicious too. I use off cuts for trifles or as tasters for willing kitchen helpers.

Tim's Tips

- **If you use frozen blueberries then let them defrost on the cake for 15 minutes before baking as frozen blueberries tend to float to the centre.**

- **I like an extra boost of almond flavour by using extract but this is optional you could use a little less than ½ tsp if you like a more subtle flavour.**

- **Like every cake the flavour and texture will improve if left until the next day.**

- **You could swap the blueberries for other soft berries if you prefer.**

Carrot Cake

Makes one 24cm cake

Cake
3 medium eggs
280g caster sugar
300g sunflower oil
220g plain flour
2 tsp baking powder
1 tsp bicarbonate of soda
2 tsp freshly ground cinnamon
pinch of salt
400g fresh carrot (250g grated net weight required)

Frosting
300g unsalted butter (melted and warm)
180g icing sugar
240g Philadelphia cream cheese
1 tsp vanilla extract

Roughly chopped pistachio nuts & marzipan carrots (optional)

1. Preheat the oven to 160°C (non fan oven 180°C).
2. Line 2 x 24cm spring form tins with parchment and place aside.
3. Weigh the flour, baking powder, bicarbonate of soda, salt and cinnamon.
4. Sift the dry ingredients onto a separate piece of parchment and place aside.
5. Weigh the caster sugar in a bowl and place aside.
6. Weigh the vegetable oil in a bowl and place aside.
7. Weigh 400g of carrots then peel and grate the carrots very fine.
8. Weigh 250g of prepared carrot into a bowl then place aside.
9. Place the eggs into a bowl for a stand mixer and whisk on high speed for 1 minute.
10. Gradually add the sugar and whisk on high speed until thick.
11. Trickle the oil into the bowl in a steady stream until fully blended.
12. Remove the bowl from the machine and add the dry ingredients.
13. Mix together with a hand whisk until completely blended and smooth.
14. Scrape any mixture off the whisk into the bowl.
15. Add the carrots and mix in well with a maris until the batter is lump free.
16. Place 600g of batter in each of the 2 tins.
17. Bake for 30-35 minutes or until the cakes spring back.
18. When baked remove and leave to cool in the tins for 30 minutes.
19. Place into an airtight container and leave to cool completely.
20. For the frosting melt the butter and place aside.
21. Place the icing sugar, cream cheese and vanilla into a small bowl.

22. Whisk with a hand held electric mixer until smooth.
23. Add the melted butter in one go and whisk slowly until smooth.
24. Place one sponge crust side up on the table then add 1/3rd of the frosting.
25. Spread the frosting right up the edge of the sponge.
26. Place the second sponge crust side down on top and lightly press.
27. Place the cake onto a cake board or plate before icing.
28. Cover the top and sides with the remaining frosting then smooth with a scraper.
29. Decorate the top and sides as desired then chill for 2 hours.

Carrot Cake

Carrot Cake Many years ago I had a conversation with my junior pastry chef Clare about writing books and I asked her which recipes I should publish, without thinking she said "your carrot cake". The beauty of carrot cake is that it keeps wonderfully moist. The trick is to grate the carrots very fine"nose first" through the small holes of a grater. I use sunflower oil as it has a neutral flavour. I like to make marzipan carrots and use pistachio nuts ground to a semi-powder for décor on the cake as I love the appearance the nuts give. If you prefer to avoid nuts altogether then just cover with the frosting.

The unique thing about this recipe is the method to make the cream cheese frosting. I only use Philadelphia and I always melt the butter. If you melt the butter and add to the whipped cream cheese and icing sugar at about 40°C the warm melted butter emulsifies the frosting and makes it beautifully smooth.

Tim's Tips

- **Grate the carrot finely on the small holes on the grater or the cake will be dry.**

- **The frosting is simple to make, use melted butter that is slightly warm, if it is too hot the frosting is too runny, if it's too cold the frosting seizes up.**

- **I make the marzipan carrots and dry them out on a tray for a few hours. I Place them on the cake when serving or they go too soft.**

- **I colour 120g of marzipan (recipe page 73) with orange colour. This makes 12 carrots weighed at 10g. I use halves of pistachio for the stalks.**

Chocolate Diabolo Cake

Makes one 24cm cake

Cake

270g 70% dark chocolate
270g unsalted butter
6 medium egg whites
120g caster sugar
6 medium egg yolks
60g caster sugar
90g ground almonds
45g plain flour
pinch of salt

Glaze

235g 70% dark chocolate
150g unsalted butter
35g golden syrup

Décor

20g milk chocolate melted + gold leaf (optional)

1. Preheat the oven to 170°C (non fan ovens 190°C).
2. Line a 24cm spring form tin with parchment paper and place aside.
3. Take the bowl for a stand mixer and the whisk attachment.
4. Take a large bowl and the whisk attachments for the hand held electric mixer.
5. Rinse the bowls and whisk attachments with boiling water then place aside.
6. Weigh the flour and salt in a bowl.
7. Sift onto a piece of parchment then add the ground almonds and place aside.
8. Weigh the 60g and 120g of caster sugar in two separate bowls and place aside.
9. Melt the chocolate and butter in a bowl in the microwave then place aside.
10. Place the whites into the machine bowl and the yolks in the large bowl.
11. Whisk the whites on high speed and gradually add the 120g sugar until well risen.
12. Whisk the yolks with a hand held electric mixer on high speed.
13. Gradually add the 60g of caster sugar to the yolks and whisk until thick.
14. Fold the melted butter and chocolate into the yolks and sugar with a whisk.
15. Add the flour, salt and almonds and gently fold together with a whisk until smooth.
16. Add one third of the meringue and whisk in quickly.
17. Add the remaining meringue and fold in carefully with a maris until smooth.
18. Scrape the cake batter into the tin and spread level with a spoon.
19. Bake for 40-45 minutes until lightly springy in the centre.
20. Remove from the oven and leave to cool in the tin for 20 minutes.
21. Remove from the tin but leave on the base to avoid breaking.

22. Place the cake on the base into the fridge to chill for 1 hour.
23. For the glaze place the ingredients into a large bowl.
24. Place into the microwave and melt on medium heat in 30 seconds bursts.
25. Stir together until smooth and lump free then leave aside to cool slightly.
26. When the cake is cold trim the top edge to level then turn over onto a wire rack.
27. Remove the base of the tin and the paper then brush off any crumbs with a brush.
28. Lift the cake on the wire rack over a large bowl to collect the chocolate glaze.
29. Pour the glaze over the cake and repeat until nicely coated then place aside.
30. Melt the milk chocolate in a small bowl then place into a paper piping cornet.
31. Pipe lines of milk chocolate over the cake then chill in the fridge for 30 minutes.
32. Slide a knife dipped in hot water under the cake to release from the wire rack.
33. Lift carefully onto a plate or cake card and decorate as desired.

Diabolo in Spanish means "devil" so this is a version of a devil's food cake but more refined and decadent with a gorgeous soft bitter-sweet icing. This cake should definitely not be overbaked. If you bake it slightly either side of 40 minutes you should be fine. The separate whisking of the yolks and whites creates a lot of air so the crust is biscuit like. The cake will sink in the middle a little post baking and this is exactly how it should be, you will need to cut off the top edge to make the cake level before turning over.

It's best to place the cake in the fridge to chill still on the base of the tin to avoid breaking it. The excess sponge is easy to cut off once the cake is cold. I always flip the sponge over as the bottom has sharp corners which makes a neater top when glazed.

Tim's Tips

- **Always rinse the bowls & whisks to be used with boiling water.**
- **Use at least 70% dark chocolate. I use St Domingue or Tanzania.**
- **The cake glazes best when cold and the icing warm.**
- **I like lines of milk chocolate and a fleck of gold leaf for a bit of luxury.**
- **To cut portions use a flat bladed knife dipped in very hot water.**

Coffee & Walnut Cake

Makes one 20cm cake

Cake
100g unsalted butter
100g icing sugar
6 medium egg yolks
40g plain flour
1 tsp baking powder
150g chopped walnuts (blitzed roughly in a food processor)
4 medium egg whites
60g caster sugar
2 tsp coffee extract
Coffee Syrup
70g strong black coffee
70g caster sugar
coffee extract to taste (optional)
Buttercream
1 batch of Italian buttercream (page 77)
coffee extract, espresso & kahlua liquor to taste
Toasted walnuts & melted dark chocolate to decorate

1. Preheat the oven to 170°C (non fan oven 190°C).
2. Line 2 x 20cm loose bottomed tins with parchment and place aside.
3. Weigh the flour and baking powder then sift onto parchment.
4. Add the blitzed walnuts to the flour and baking powder then place aside.
5. Place the butter and icing sugar into the bowl for a stand mixer.
6. Cream together on medium speed with the whisk attachment for 4-5 minutes.
7. Add the egg yolks in about 3 additions whisking in well each time.
8. Add the coffee extract and mix in well.
9. Remove the bowl from the machine and scrape down.
10. Add the flour, baking powder and walnuts and fold together gently with a maris.
11. Place the whites into a bowl for a stand mixer and whisk on high speed.
12. Gradually add the 60g of caster sugar and whisk until you form a soft meringue.
13. Add one third of the meringue to the bowl and mix in briskly with a hand whisk.
14. Add the remainder of the meringue and fold in carefully with a maris until smooth.
15. Place 320g of batter into each tin and spread level with a spoon.
16. Bake for 15-20 minutes until the sponges are springy.
17. Remove from the oven and cover with a clean tea towel until cold.
18. Make the coffee syrup and flavour as desired.

19. Make the buttercream (page 77) then add the coffee extract and espresso to taste.
20. Turn the sponges onto a sheet of parchment paper.
21. Carefully brush the sponges well with the syrup on both sides.
22. Place one third of the coffee buttercream on one of the sponges.
23. Place the other sponge on top and lightly press the sponges together.
24. Spread half the remaining buttercream neatly on the top and sides.
25. Place the remaining buttercream into a piping bag.
26. Decorate the top edge of the cake with piped buttercream.
27. Decorate with toasted walnuts and melted chocolate as desired.

Coffee is a great passion of mine as anyone who knows me well will confirm, I even describe myself as a coffee snob on my Twitter profile. Coffee of course is wonderful paired with walnuts in a cake and every pastry chef or baker I know has their own version of a coffee & walnut cake. I use a slightly unusual method to make my walnut sponge in that I use a "split method" which means I whisk the egg whites separately then add to the cake batter last which makes a light but nutty walnut sponge.

I use my basic Italian buttercream recipe flavoured with fresh espresso and coffee extract and lightly soak the sponge with a coffee syrup, the Kahlua liquor in the syrup is optional but I like a splash in mine. The syrup also preserves the cake and extends the shelf life as well as making the texture moist and beautiful to eat. Give this version a try there is a bit of work involved but the end result is gorgeous.

Tim's Tips
- **I pulse the walnuts in a food processor to break them up. Don't make them too small they should be small chunks roughly ½ cm in size.**

- **I use freshly made espresso if you don't have a machine make a very strong cafetière coffee or a paste with instant coffee and boiled water.**

- **The buttercream is light and smooth and worth the trouble to make it.**

- **I like a strong coffee flavour but make to your own personal taste.**

Devil's Food Cake
Makes one 20 cm cake

Ganache
110g whipping cream
200g softened unsalted butter
260g 70% dark chocolate
Chocolate Sponges
60g cocoa powder
280g boiling water
1 tsp vanilla extract
110g light brown sugar
250g plain flour
¾ tsp baking powder
¾ tsp bicarbonate of soda
150g unsalted butter
130g caster sugar
3 medium eggs

1. Preheat the oven to 170°C (non fan oven 190°C).
2. Place the cocoa powder into a bowl with the brown sugar and vanilla.
3. Pour 280g of boiling water into the bowl.
4. Whisk together until smooth and lump free then place aside to cool.
5. Make the chocolate ganache first by boiling the cream in a bowl in the microwave.
6. Add the chocolate and butter then heat for 30 seconds further in the microwave.
7. Mix until smooth then leave aside to cool stirring occasionally with a maris.
8. Line 3 x 20cm loose bottomed tins with parchment and place aside.
9. Weigh the flour, baking powder and bicarbonate of soda in a bowl.
10. Sift the dry ingredients onto a separate piece of parchment paper and place aside.
11. Place the butter and caster sugar into the bowl for a stand mixer.
12. Cream with the whisk attachment for 5-6 minutes until light.
13. Add the eggs one at a time beating each in well until smooth then scrape down.
14. Add the dry ingredients and mix very slowly on the slowest speed until smooth.
15. When the mixture comes together add the cooled cocoa mixture.
16. Mix slowly for 30 seconds just to combine.
17. Remove the bowl from the machine and mix through with a maris until smooth.
18. When the batter is lump free and smooth place 365g of mix into each tin.
19. Bake for 20-25 minutes or until the sponges are springy.
20. Leave to cool in the tins for 30 minutes covered with clean tea towels.
21. The ganache should be thick enough to spread by now, if it's not chill briefly.

22. Level the sponges with a sharp serrated knife.
23. Place a sponge onto a cake card or plate.
24. Place about a quarter of the ganache on the first sponge.
25. Spread to the edges in a nice thin even layer coming slightly over the edges.
26. Place the second sponge on top press lightly together.
27. Repeat with the ganache then place the third sponge on top upside down.
28. Lightly press down to level the cake, if using place the cake onto a turntable.
29. Place all of the remaining ganache on top of the cake.
30. Spread the ganache evenly over the top and sides of the cake.
31. Make marks on the frosting with a knife or spoon to your preference.
32. Place into the fridge for 30 minutes to slightly firm up the ganache.
33. Lightly dust the centre with icing sugar.

Devil's Food Cake is one of my favourite chocolate cakes and one that could also be used for a birthday cake or as a dessert. The unique aspect of this sponge is that the chocolate element for the sponge is cocoa powder blended with boiled water and brown sugar which results a light sticky chocolate sponge. The cake is layered and covered with a totally addictive chocolate ganache. You will need to trim the sponges slightly as the cakes peak in the oven. Take care to get the ganache to a nice consistency as it needs to be firm enough to spread. I like to run a palette knife up the sides to texture the sides on a cake turntable but this is an optional flourish.

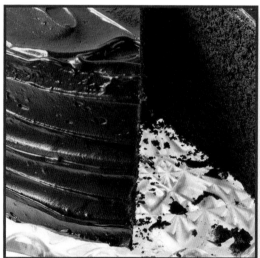

Tim's Tips

- **Your sponges should have a slight peak after baking so level with a knife.**

- **Only assemble when the sponges are cold and the ganache is a nice spreadable consistency.**

- **Portion the cake with a flat bladed knife dipped in hot water.**

- **Store the cake in the fridge but take out an hour before serving to allow to come back to room temperature for maximum flavour and a soft icing.**

Flourless Chocolate Cake

Makes one 24cm cake

Cake
190g unsalted butter
190g 70% dark chocolate
5 medium eggs
90g caster sugar
60g caster sugar
70g ground almonds
30g cocoa powder
pinch salt
Decoration
3 tsp good quality cocoa powder mixed with ½ tsp icing sugar

1. Preheat the oven to 180°C (non fan oven 200°C).
2. Line a 24cm spring form tin with parchment paper and place aside.
3. Take the bowl for a stand mixer and the whisk attachment.
4. Take a large bowl and the whisk attachments for the hand held electric mixer.
5. Rinse the bowls and whisk attachments with boiled water then place aside.
6. Weigh the cocoa powder, salt and ground almonds together in a bowl.
7. Weigh the 90g and 60g of caster sugar in two separate bowls and place aside.
8. Melt the butter and chocolate together in a bowl in the microwave.
9. Separate the 5 eggs and place the whites into the bowl for a stand mixer.
10. Place the yolks into a large bowl and place aside.
11. Whisk the whites on medium speed gradually adding the 90g of sugar.
12. When the meringue is at soft peaks remove from the machine and place aside.
13. Meanwhile with a hand held electric beater whisk the yolks on medium speed.
14. Gradually add the 60g of sugar and whisk until risen and quite pale.
15. Fold the melted butter and chocolate into the yolks and sugar until blended.
16. Add the cocoa powder, salt and ground almonds and fold in with a whisk.
17. Add one third of the meringue and whisk in briskly.
18. Fold in the remainder of the meringue carefully with a maris.
19. Place the mix into the tin and spread level.
20. Bake for 20-25 minutes or until springy in the centre.
21. Remove from the oven and leave to cool In the tin for 30 minutes.
22. Remove the tin leave on the base and place into the fridge to chill for 1 hour.
23. Remove the cake from the base and place into a container on a cake card.
24. Before serving dust lightly with the cocoa powder and icing sugar.

Flourless Chocolate Cakes became quite fashionable in the 1990's and were often found in trendy cafés and patisseries. The beauty of these cakes apart from being gluten free is that they were gooey in the centre which made them ideal desserts. This version is no exception and has a deceptively light texture more reminiscent of a chocolate mousse with a lovely firm outer crust. The flour content of this recipe is replaced with a mixture of ground almonds and dark cocoa powder which adds a further depth of chocolate flavour. I use either a 70% St Domingue or Amedei chocolate for this or if I want a more bitter version 75% Tanzanian dark.

The aeration for this cake comes from separating the eggs then whisking the yolks and whites with sugar to incorporate lots of air. This method makes the cake soufflé up in the oven and then slightly fall back on itself. The cake must be under-baked to retain the typical soft interior so adjust the baking time to your personal taste. The finished cake is simply decorated with a dusting of cocoa powder and icing sugar mixed together. I like this served as a cake with a coffee or as a dessert slightly warm with a big dollop of clotted cream and perhaps some fruit.

Tim's Tips

- I melt my chocolate and butter in a bowl in the microwave but you can place into a heatproof bowl and melt over a pan of water if you prefer.

- Buy the darkest best quality cocoa powder you can find for best results.

- I whisk my eggs whites in a stand mixer and the yolks in a bowl with a hand held electric whisk. If you only have one machine, whisk the whites first place aside then whisk the yolks next to avoid rewashing the whisk.

- If you wish to serve it warm as a dessert heat individual portions on a plate for 20 seconds in the microwave to make it warm and gooey.

Genoa Fruit Cake

Makes 24 pieces

60g candied lemon peel
180g glacé cherries
180g sultanas
100g mini currants
165g unsalted butter
165g caster sugar
½ tsp lemon extract
¼ tsp almond extract
½ tsp vanilla extract
zest of 1 lemon
4 medium eggs
235g plain flour
2 tsp baking powder
2 tsp glycerine

1. Preheat the oven to 150°C (non fan 170°C).
2. Chop the lemon peel into ½ cm pieces then place into a bowl.
3. If the cherries are whole cut them in half then add to the lemon peel.
4. Pour hot water (about 70°C) onto the lemon and cherries and soak for 10 minutes.
5. Line a 24cm square tin with a double lining of parchment and place aside.
6. Weigh the caster sugar and place aside.
7. Weigh the flour and baking powder then sieve into a stand mixer bowl.
8. Drain the cherries and peel through a sieve then gently squeeze out the excess water.
9. Place the fruit onto a cloth and rub dry then place into a bowl.
10. Add the sultanas and currants to the cherries and peel.
11. Take one spoon of the dry ingredients from the machine bowl and add to the fruit.
12. Mix together until all the fruit has been coated with the dry ingredients.
13. Place the prepared fruit to one side.
14. Add the butter to the machine bowl and mix slowly until combined.
15. Beat well on medium for 4-5 minutes until very light then scrape down.
16. Add the lemon zest, flavours and glycerine to the flour and butter.
17. Place the eggs into a clean medium sized bowl.
18. Whisk on high speed with a hand held electric mixer.
19. Gradually add all the 165g of caster sugar and whisk until thick and well risen.
20. Add a quarter of the eggs and sugar to the machine bowl and mix in well.
21. Add the remaining eggs and sugar in three additions mixing each in well.
22. Scrape down the machine bowl to ensure all the batter is well mixed.
23. Mix the cake batter for 3 minutes on medium speed to strengthen.

24. Add the fruit and mix in slowly for 20 seconds until well combined.
25. Scrape the batter into the cake tin and flatten with a damp hand.
26. Place a shallow pan of water into the base of the oven.
27. Load the cake onto the middle shelf of the oven.
28. Bake at for 70-80 minutes or until the centre is springy and firm.
29. Place a sheet of parchment paper on top of the cake.
30. Place a large tray on the parchment and carefully turn the cake over.
31 Leave the tin on top and cool on the tray for 1 hour.
32. Remove the tin and lift the cake on the paper into an airtight container.
33. The next day lift the cake out of the container.
34. Remove the four edges of the cake then cut the cake into 3 even strips.
35. Cut each strip into 8 slices.

Genoa fruit cake is a classic slab cake originating from a recipe in Italy which has been much adapted from the original. It contains dried fruits and is usually perfumed with vanilla, almond and lemon. This is a medium heavy fruited cake and made using the flour batter method which is a fairly normal procedure for slab cakes. The advantage of this method is that it produces a fine textured cake that remains light and soft whilst being strong enough to hold the fruit up in the cake. I prefer to use Whitworth's mini currants and their excellent sultanas. The cake takes at least an hour to bake so I double line the tin with parchment paper to ensure the crust does not colour too much.

Tim's Tips

- **The mini currants and sunshine sultanas do not need soaking but if you can't get hold of them buy the best quality you can find and soak with the lemon peel and cherries then drain and dry thoroughly on a tea towel.**

- **The long mixing is essential for the fine texture and to ensure the fruit does not sink in the cake.**

- **Glycerine is a humectant and helps to extend the shelf life. It is quite easy to find in the supermarket but if you cannot get it just leave it out it's fine.**

- **I always flip the cake over onto a paper lined tray to cool as this helps keep the crust soft and flattens the top making the cake portions even when cut.**

Ginger Loaf Cake

Makes one loaf cake

30g stem ginger paste
(made from whole jar of stem ginger including the syrup see point 3 below)
150g plain flour
1 tsp baking powder
3½ tsp ground ginger
1 tsp ground cinnamon
60g unsalted butter
120g golden syrup
25g honey
85g light brown sugar
30g finely grated fresh ginger
80g whole milk
1 medium egg

1. Preheat the oven to 150°C (non fan oven 170°C).
2. Line a 1lb loaf tin with parchment paper or a cake liner and place aside.
3. Place the entire contents of a jar of stem ginger in syrup into a food processor.
4. Blitz until smooth then scrape back into the jar and store in the fridge.
5. Weigh the flour, baking powder and spices.
6. Sift onto a piece of separate parchment and place aside.
7. Place the butter, golden syrup, honey and brown sugar into a bowl.
8. Heat in the microwave on medium for 1 minute then whisk until smooth.
9. Peel the fresh ginger and grate very finely and place into a bowl (I use a microplane).
10. Whisk in the fresh ginger and 30g of the prepared ginger paste until smooth.
11. Whisk in the milk then add the egg and whisk until the batter is smooth.
12. Add the dry ingredients and mix in with a whisk until lump free and smooth.
13. Scrape the batter carefully into the lined loaf tin.
14. Place into the oven and bake for 45-50 minutes.
15. When the cake springs back remove from the oven and place aside for 1 hour.
16. Lift the cake from the tin still in the paper.
17. Place into an airtight container to mature and soften.
18. Leave for at least 24 to 48 hours.
19. Remove the end crusts and then cut the cake into 8 even slices.

Ginger always gives me fond memories of the loaf cakes made by Mcvities. My mum would often buy the golden syrup or ginger ones for tea on Sundays. My main memory is that both were moist and sweet and went fantastically well with a cup of tea. I am not a big fan of super-hot ginger cakes with black treacle and dark brown sugar, I prefer mine sticky and sweet but with a good warmth of ginger coming through. I have used stem ginger as a puree for years it adds a great flavour to sauces and puddings. The syrup and the ginger pieces blend into a lovely paste with a great balance of heat and sweetness which is a great stand by ingredient to have in the fridge.

The cake is definitely not a light and fluffy product but a sticky and fairly dense cake albeit with a soft texture and sticky crust. This cake only rises slightly in the centre so do not expect a towering peaked cake. The cake contains a high level of sugars and quite a lot of milk and therefore needs to be baked out slowly. I tweaked this recipe many times before I got to the result that I was happy with. This cake tastes and eats amazing well after sitting in an airtight box for 2 days. I would go as far to say that eating it in the first day or perhaps even the second would be disappointing so be patient and wait for the best results.

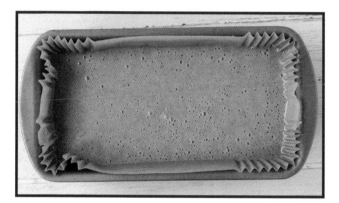 

Tim's Tips

- I use a large plastic bowl to warm the sugar, golden syrup and butter as I find this easier to combine the other ingredients to but you could use a pan.

- I use whole milk but semi skimmed is ok and makes very little difference.

- I love the flavour of the ginger paste with the fresh and powdered ginger as it gives the cake a lovely rounded ginger flavour.

- I add a little honey as I like the subtle flavour this adds.

- I use ground cinnamon with the ginger as I think it improves the flavour.

- If you like a very hot ginger cake you could add another tsp of ground ginger. For me the cake is just right but adjust to your own personal taste.

Hazelnut Chocolate Cake

Makes one 20cm cake

Cake

180g 70% dark chocolate

180g unsalted butter

4 medium eggs

120g caster sugar

60g ground hazelnuts

30g plain flour

pinch of salt

250g chocolate hazelnut paste

(Home-made page 75) or bought

Hazelnut Brittle

30g caster sugar

60g blanched peeled hazelnuts

1. Preheat the oven to 180°C (non fan oven 200°C).
2. Take the bowl for a stand mixer and the whisk attachment.
3. Take a large bowl and the whisk attachments for the hand held electric mixer.
4. Rinse the bowls and whisk attachments with boiling water then place aside.
5. Line a 20cm spring form tin with parchment paper and place aside.
6. For the hazelnut brittle weigh the 60g of blanched whole hazelnuts.
7. Place onto a parchment lined tray and bake for 6-8 minutes.
8. Place an empty pan onto the heat to get hot.
9. Gradually add the 30g of sugar to make a dry amber coloured caramel (page 76).
10. Add the hot golden hazelnuts and stir together carefully until well coated.
11. Tip the nuts onto a sheet of parchment and leave aside to cool.
12. When cool place into an airtight box, reduce the oven to 170°C (non fan oven 190°C).
13. Weigh the flour and salt then sift onto parchment.
14. Add the ground hazelnuts and place aside.
15. Melt the chocolate and butter in a bowl in the microwave mix well then place aside.
16. Separate the eggs, place the whites into the machine bowl and the yolks a large bowl.
17. Whisk the whites on high speed gradually adding 2/3rds of the 120g of caster sugar.
18. Whisk until the meringue forms soft peaks then leave running on the lowest speed.
19. In the large rinsed bowl place the yolks and whisk on high speed with the hand mixer.
20. Gradually add the remaining sugar and whisk until thick and well risen.
21. Turn the meringue off and remove the bowl from the machine.
22. Fold the butter and chocolate into the yolks and sugar with a whisk until smooth.
23. Add the flour, salt and ground hazelnuts and fold in with a whisk until smooth.
24. Add one third of the meringue and whisk in quickly.
25. Add the remaining meringue and fold in carefully with a maris until smooth.

26. Scrape the batter into the tin and spread level with a spoon.
27. Bake for 30-35 minutes until lightly springy in the centre.
28. Remove from the oven and leave to cool in the tin for 30 minutes.
29. Remove from the tin but leave on the base to avoid breaking.
30. Place into the fridge for 1 hour to chill completely.
31. When cold cut off the top crust and turn over carefully onto a plate or cake card.
32. Brush off any crumbs with a dry clean pastry brush.
33. Spoon the chocolate hazelnut paste onto the top of the cake.
34. Spread the paste evenly over the top and down the sides with a palette knife.
35. Place the hazelnut brittle into a freezer bag and smash with a heavy pan.
36. Sprinkle the hazelnut brittle over the top of the cake.
37. Place into the fridge to set for 1 hour.

Hazelnut and chocolate is a classic combination, after all who doesn't like Nutella? I prefer to make my own as I find the shop bought one a bit too sweet. I also have a bit of an issue using palm oil so if you feel the same way then try the home-made recipe on page 75. The cake requires ground hazelnuts which can easily be bought through many online stores. The ground hazelnuts are essential not only for the flavour of the cake but also the texture as the oil in the nuts add a nice texture to the finished cake. If you can't get hold of ground hazelnuts you could use ground almonds they will work fine for this cake but the flavour will be slightly less pronounced.

Like all chocolate cakes this needs to be under-baked. I also like the hazelnut brittle quite small, the best way to break it up is to put the brittle in a freezer bag and break with the base of a saucepan. See page 76 for information on how to make a dry caramel.

Tim's Tips

- Take care to rinse the bowls and whisks with boiling water to ensure you remove any grease so that the eggs whisk up well.

- The cake needs to be under-baked if in doubt take it out early it's better to have a gooey cake than a dry one.

- I use 70% dark St Domingue but a good quality blended chocolate is fine.

- Place the cake into the fridge to set the icing but take out an hour before serving as the cake taste much better at room temperature.

Honey Cake

Makes 16 pieces of cake

130g unsalted butter
200g clear honey
100g soft light brown sugar
3 medium eggs
3 tsp whole milk
225g plain flour
2 tsp baking powder
70g raw flaked almonds
120g honey to brush over

1. Preheat the oven to 170°C (non fan oven 190°C).
2. Line a 30cm x 20cm brownie tin with parchment paper and place aside.
3. Weigh the flour and baking powder in a small bowl.
4. Sift the dry ingredients onto a separate piece of parchment paper and place aside.
5. Melt the butter in a large bowl then add the honey and brown sugar.
6. Whisk together until smooth and the all of the sugar has dissolved.
7. Whisk in the milk then the eggs one at a time until well combined.
8. Add the dry ingredients and mix in with a maris until smooth.
9. When the batter lump free scrape into the tin.
10. Sprinkle the flaked almonds evenly over the cake.
11. Bake for 20-25 minutes until golden and springy.
12. Meanwhile boil the honey in a small bowl in the microwave.
13. As soon as the cake is springy remove from the oven and brush with the hot honey.
14. Leave to cool in the tin for 1 hour.
15. Remove the cake from the tin still in the paper and place into an airtight container.
16. When cold remove the edges and cut in 16 pieces (4 x 4).

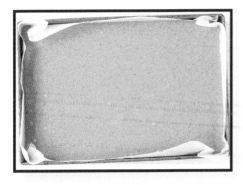

Honey is a difficult thing to use in cakes as it burns easily and an excess can make the recipe unbalanced as honey is the sweetest natural food. The solution I found was to add some to the recipe but also to brush honey over the top of the hot cake. This not only adds more honey flavour but helps keep the crust nice and soft. I tried this in a round cake tin but the extra time baking the denser cake resulted in an unpleasantly thick crust.

I bake mine in a brownie tin as this reduces the baking time resulting in a soft sticky cake with a thin crust. All cakes moisten up after a day or so but cakes with honey and syrups even more so. This cake eats beautifully after 24 hours and goes perfectly with tea particularly Earl Grey. I like to sprinkle flaked almonds over the top as they go so well with the honey, you could swap them for pine nuts or leave them out completely if you wish to avoid nuts. A very simple cake to make and very hard to eat just one piece!

Tim's Tips

- **I use clear honey for this, there is no need to use an expensive one, I like orange blossom or acacia honey.**

- **Brush the honey over the cake as soon as it comes out of the oven using it all up.**

- **Bake the cake until it just springs back do not overcook or it will be dry.**

- **Don't be tempted to cut the cake too early it's lovely 24 hours after baking.**

Iced Vanilla Cake

Makes one loaf cake

Cake
**80g unsalted Butter
(softened)
120g plain flour
1¼ tsp baking powder
1 tsp glycerine
1 tsp vanilla extract
1 vanilla pod
2 medium eggs
80g caster sugar
1 tsp whole milk**

Icing
**30g water
30g caster sugar
75g sieved icing sugar**

1. Preheat the oven to 170°C (non fan oven 190°C).
2. Line a 1lb loaf tin with parchment paper or cake liner and place aside.
3. Sieve the flour and baking powder into the bowl for a stand mixer.
4. Add the butter and mix together with the beater attachment slowly for 1 minute.
5. Split the vanilla pod down the centre and scrape out the seeds.
6. Add the seeds to the machine bowl with the glycerine and vanilla extract.
7. Beat on medium speed for 4-5 minutes until light.
8. Weigh 80g of sugar in a small bowl and place aside.
9. Place the eggs into a bowl and whisk on high speed.
10. Gradually add the sugar whisking until thick and well risen.
11. Add a quarter of the sugar and eggs to the machine bowl and beat in for 1 minute.
12. Add the remaining eggs and sugar to the bowl in 3 additions mixing in each well.
13. When adding the last batch of sugar and eggs scrape down the machine bowl.
14. Mix briefly on medium speed until the batter is smooth.
15. Remove from the machine and add the milk then mix with a maris until smooth.
16. Scrape the batter into the loaf tin and spread level with a spoon.
17. Bake for 30-35 minutes until the sponge springs back.
18. Meanwhile make the syrup for the icing, place the vanilla pod into a small pan.
19. Add the 30g of sugar and 30g of water and bring up to the boll.
20. Stir together until the sugar dissolves then place aside to infuse for 30 minutes.
21. When the cake springs back remove from the oven.
22. Leave to cool in the tin covered with a tea towel for 20 minutes.

23. To make the icing re-boil the sugar, water and vanilla.
24. Sieve the icing sugar into a bowl then strain the syrup on top.
25. Mix well until a smooth icing is formed.
26. Pour onto the cake in the tin spreading evenly over the top into the corners.
27. Leave to dry completely in the tin then store in an airtight container.
28. To serve remove the cake from the tin and peel off the paper.
29. Cut the two ends off the cake then cut into 8 -10 slices.

Vanilla is seldom used as the main flavouring for a cake as it can be quite difficult to capture the flavour. This is perhaps the simplest cake in the book but not as simple to make as you may think. This is another example of the flour batter method of cake making. The dry ingredients are beaten with the butter until pale and very light in consistency. The eggs and sugar are whisked to a light sabayon then gradually added to the flour and butter. The long beating process incorporates a lot of air in the mixture creating a light but tightly textured cake. This version is vanilla all the way with a lovely sweet dry icing just to give a little extra dimension to the cake.

Tim's Tips

- **The quality of this cake depends almost entirely on the beating so take care to do this carefully and scrape down inbetween.**

- **If you prefer to make a Madeira cake, omit the vanilla pod and use the zest of 1 lemon and a little vanilla, almond and lemon extracts.**

- **Glycerine is a humectant and helps to extend the shelf life. It is quite easy to find in the supermarket but if you cannot get it just leave it out it's fine.**

- **Most of the flavour in vanilla is actually in the pods and not the seeds, by using the pod to make the syrup and the seeds in the cake you get the maximum flavour out of the very expensive pod.**

- **Wash the pods then dry them out and reuse. Alternatively dried pods added to a pot of sugar makes lovely vanilla sugar.**

Lemon Cake

Makes one 20cm cake

Cake
40g unsalted butter
110g plain flour
½ tsp baking powder
2 medium eggs
140g caster sugar
finely grated zest of 5 lemons
½ tsp lemon extract
60g whipping cream
Syrup
55g lemon juice
100g caster sugar
Icing
25g lemon juice
85g sifted icing sugar

1. Preheat the oven to 170°C (non fan oven 190°C).
2. Line a 20cm loose bottomed tin with parchment paper and place aside.
3. Weigh the flour and baking powder in a small bowl.
4. Sift the dry ingredients onto a separate piece of parchment and place aside.
5. Zest the lemons with the fine side of a grater then place the zest into a large bowl.
6. Squeeze the juice from the lemons through a sieve into a bowl then place aside.
7. Melt the butter in a small bowl in the microwave then place aside.
8. Place the extract, eggs and sugar in the large bowl with the zest and whisk together.
9. Add the cream and carefully mix in with the whisk until completely blended.
10. Add the melted warm butter and mix in with the whisk.
11. Add the sifted dry ingredients and whisk together carefully until smooth.
12. Gently mix with a maris until smooth then scrape the batter into the tin.
13. Bake for 20-25 minutes or until the cake springs back.
14. Leave the cake to settle in the tin for 5 minutes.
15. Place 55g of the lemon juice into a plastic bowl with the 100g of caster sugar.
16. Boil in the microwave for 1 minute then mix until the sugar has dissolved.
17. Carefully remove the cake from the tin and place onto a wire rack over a plate.
18. Skewer the cake all over 20-30 times then brush the top and sides with the hot syrup.
19. Repeat until all of the syrup has been used up.

20. Leave on the wire rack while you make the lemon icing.
21. Weigh the icing sugar then sift onto a piece of parchment paper and place aside.
22. Using the same bowl used for the syrup weigh the 25g of lemon juice.
23. Boil in the microwave briefly then add the icing sugar and mix with a maris.
24. When the icing is smooth brush the icing over the top and sides of the cake.
25. Leave the cake to dry on the wire rack for 30 minutes.
26. Carefully remove the cake from the wire rack and place onto a plate or cake card.
27. Store in an airtight container for 24 hours.
28. Cut by dipping a flat bladed knife into very hot water.

Lemon cake is one of my all time favourites and after much experimentation I have arrived at what I think is the ultimate recipe. Blissfully this cake is very easy to make and can be made by hand in a large bowl. This cake is made very much in the French style and includes lots of lemons and a little cream which adds moisture and richness and rounds off the lemon flavour beautifully.

The trick is to brush the top and sides of the warm cake with the hot lemon syrup and then brush the lemon water icing over the top and sides so the icing dries to a glassy crust. The crust gives the cake a simple but elegant appearance with a sharp lemon bite. Make sure you brush the icing on while fairly hot or it won't dry out properly. You will find that most of the flavour of the cake comes from the crust. The cake is fairly flat, giving a good ratio of crust to crumb giving a big hit of lemon flavour.

Tim's Tips

- As with all citrus fruits, grate using the finest side of a grater.

- Leave the cake for 24 hours to allow the flavour to really come through.

- I use standard sized unwaxed lemons as they taste a lot better.

- If you cannot get unwaxed lemons wash standard lemons briefly in hot water and wipe them dry with a clean tea towel.

Lime & Coconut Cake

Makes 16 pieces of cake

Cake
150g unsalted butter (softened)
150g caster sugar
½ tsp coconut flavour
3 medium eggs
zest of 8 limes
150g plain flour
50g desiccated coconut
1 tsp baking powder
Lime syrup
30g lime juice
50g caster sugar
Lime water icing
40g lime juice
80g icing sugar (sifted)
Topping
30g desiccated coconut

1. Preheat the oven to 170°C (non fan oven 190°C).
2. Line a 30cm x 20cm brownie tin with parchment paper and place aside.
3. Weigh the flour and baking powder in a bowl.
4. Sift onto a separate piece of parchment paper and place aside.
5. Blitz the coconut briefly then add to the sifted ingredients and place aside.
6. Place the butter, sugar, zest and flavour into a bowl for a stand mixer.
7. Cream with the whisk attachment for 3-4 minutes until light.
8. Add the eggs one at a time beating in each well until smooth.
9. Remove the bowl from the machine and place aside.
10. Add the dry ingredients and fold together with a maris until smooth.
11. Scrape the mixture into the tin and spread level.
12. Bake for 18-22 minutes until springy.
13. For the lime syrup, place the lime juice in a small bowl with the 50g of sugar.
14. Boil in the microwave then stir together until the sugar has all dissolved.
15. When baked immediately brush the cake with the lime syrup using all of it up.
16. For the lime water ice, place the lime juice in the same bowl used for the syrup.
17. Weigh the 80g of icing sugar and sift onto a piece of parchment and place aside.
18. Bring the lime juice to the boil in the microwave and add the sifted icing sugar.
19. Stir together until smooth and lump free then scrape the icing over the cake.

20. Spread carefully over the cake with a palette knife covering all of the surface.
21. Sprinkle the 30g of coconut over the icing immediately.
22. Place aside to cool for 30 minutes then lift the cake out with the paper.
23. Place into an airtight box until the next day.
24. To serve, trim off the edges and cut the cake into 16 pieces (4 x 4).

Lime is my very favourite flavour in the kitchen and I was determined to make a new cake using it. I decided to pair it with another favourite flavour of mine coconut. I prefer the cake as a traybake type cake as it cooks quicker and therefore does not dry out. I make a lime syrup from the juice of the limes and brush over the cake as soon as it leaves the oven and then finish this off with a lime water ice. This has a dual purpose, firstly it keeps the crust of the cake beautifully moist and secondly it adds a lovely sharp zingy lime flavour to the cake.

Most coconut available is fairly coarse so I place mine into a spice grinder or food processor to make finer as I find the chunkiness of the coconut not very pleasant in the cake. I do however leave the coconut for the top a bit coarser as this adds a nice contrast. The 8 limes give the cake an incredible zesty punch which I enhance with a little coconut flavour which is easily available from most supermarkets or online food suppliers.

Tim's Tips

- **Use the finest side of the grater to zest the limes but be careful not to grate too much white pith as this is quite bitter.**

- **I blitz the coconut in a spice grinder then add to the flour and baking powder but a food processor works just fine if you don't have one.**

- **I prefer to make my lime syrup in a small bowl in the microwave but a pan works just fine if you don't have one.**

- **The coconut flavour adds another depth of flavour but it's optional.**

- **I make the lime syrup in a plastic bowl then use the same bowl to make the water icing as I find that easier.**

Macadamia Fudge Brownies

Makes 24 brownies

Brownie
250g macadamia nuts
250g unsalted butter
250g 70% dark chocolate
450g dark brown sugar
4 medium eggs
150g plain flour
2 tsp baking powder
pinch of salt
Ganache
100g whipping cream
40g unsalted butter
150g 70% dark chocolate
20g golden syrup

1. Preheat the oven to 160°C (non fan oven 180°C).
2. Line a 30cm x 20cm brownie tin with parchment paper and place aside.
3. Place the macadamia nuts onto a parchment lined baking sheet.
4. Bake for 8-10 minutes stirring occasionally until a light golden brown.
5. Place aside to cool for 10 minutes while you make the brownie.
6. Weigh the flour, baking powder and salt then sift onto parchment and place aside.
7. Melt the butter and chocolate together carefully in a bowl in the microwave.
8. Place the brown sugar and eggs into a bowl for a stand mixer.
9. Mix with the beater attachment for 2-3 minutes on medium speed until light.
10. Add the melted butter and chocolate and mix in on slow speed until smooth.
11. Remove the bowl from the machine and scrape off the beater into the bowl.
12. Add the dry ingredients and toasted macadamia nuts to the bowl.
13. Mix slowly together with a maris until smooth and completely blended.
14. Scrape the mixture into the tin and spread level.
15. Bake for 40 minutes then check the brownie colour and turn the tray if necessary.
16. Bake for a further 10-15 minutes until the brownie lightly springs back.
17. Cool in the tin for 30 minutes then turn over onto a paper lined baking tray.
18. Press the edges with the heel of your hand to flatten the brownie and make level.
19. Place a sheet of parchment on top then place a baking tray on top.
20. Flip the tray over and place the brownie into the fridge for 1 hour to chill.
21. For the ganache topping, boil the cream in a bowl in the microwave.
22. Add the butter, chocolate and golden syrup and leave for 1 minute to warm up.

23. Stir together with a maris until smooth and shiny.
24. Spread the ganache evenly over the brownie then place into the fridge for 1 hour.
25. Using a flat bladed knife dipped in hot water remove the edges.
26. Cut the brownie into 24 pieces (6 x 4).

Macadamia nuts are my favourite variety of nut and go fantastically well with all things chocolate. If the other brownie recipe is the standard then this one with macadamia nuts and a soft bitter chocolate ganache is the Rolls Royce version. If you want to give someone the ultimate chocolate treat this is the one. The baking is the same as the standard one so adjust to your preference of gooeyness.

I press the edges to make the brownie as flat as possible for even pieces and then place into the fridge to chill as this helps the ganache set. To avoid splitting the ganache the most essential step is to leave the warm ingredients together for 1 minute in the bowl before mixing. This ensures that the ingredients are roughly the same temperature when mixed so that they are shiny and smooth when combined.

Tim's Tips

- It's essential to toast the nuts before you make the brownie or the nuts will have little flavour and be soft and chewy.

- The baking of the brownie is hard to judge but whatever you do don't over-bake or your brownie will be dry and crumbly.

- Other nuts can be used, walnuts, pecans and hazelnuts are all lovely.

- I like to use a microwave to make my ganaches. If you do not have one place the chocolate and butter into a bowl then boil the cream in a pan and pour on top then proceed as instructed in the recipe.

- I like to remove the edges before cutting into 24 squares, the trimmings are fantastic in ice cream or cheesecakes cut into small chunks.

Marmalade Cake

Makes one 20cm cake

Cake
40g unsalted butter
110g plain flour
½ tsp baking powder
2 medium eggs
140g caster sugar
zest of 4 medium oranges
60g whipping cream
Syrup
100g orange juice
50g caster sugar
Glaze
100g Bonne Maman marmalade

1. Preheat the oven to 170°C (non fan ovens 190°C).
2. Line a 20cm loose bottomed tin with parchment paper and place aside.
3. Weigh the flour and baking powder in a bowl.
4. Sieve onto a separate piece of parchment and place aside.
5. Melt the butter and place aside.
6. Place the sugar in a large bowl with the orange zest.
7. Add the eggs and whisk briskly for 30 seconds.
8. Add the cream and mix in carefully with a whisk until smooth.
9. Add the dry ingredients and fold together with a whisk until smooth and lump free.
10. Add the melted warm butter and mix in with a maris until smooth.
11. Scrape the batter into the tin.
12. Bake for 20-25 minutes or until the cake springs back.
13. Leave the cake to settle in the tin for 5 minutes.
14. Meanwhile make the syrup, place the orange juice into a pan.
15. Boil rapidly and reduce by half then add the sugar.
16. Stir together until the sugar has dissolved.
17. Remove the cake from the tin and carefully place onto a wire rack over a plate.
18. Brush the top and sides of the cake with all of the syrup.
19. Boil the marmalade in a bowl or a small pan.
20. Brush all the boiling marmalade over the top and sides of the cake using it all up.
21. Leave on the wire rack to cool for 30 minutes then place onto a cake card or plate.
22. Store in an airtight container.

Marmalade is a lovely alternative to a sweet icing to finish a cake. The punchy orange flavour of the sponge contrasts beautifully with the bitter-sweet marmalade topping. I use 4 medium oranges for the precious oil in the zest to perfume the cake and use two of the oranges to make a syrup (I drink the juice from the other two). I give the cake a dousing of orange syrup before adding a thin sticky layer of boiled marmalade to the finished cake. I prefer Bonne Maman marmalade as I think the bitter-sweet balance is just right but use your own preferred brand.

The cake sponge is quite shallow and this is deliberate. The relatively short baking time ensures that the sponge does not dry out too much and the crust is thin giving 8 even slices of soft zingy bitter-sweet cake. I have a dislike of thick cakes that take ages to bake and develop a thick crust which tend to be dry and fairly tasteless. I leave the cake ungarnished and plain letting the marmalade be the flavour that hits you when taking a bite. I adore marmalade and this simple delicious cake does not disappoint.

A certain bear from darkest Peru would approve I think.

Tim's Tips

- **The zest should be whisked into the eggs and sugar well to extract the oil from the zest giving the maximum flavour.**

- **Take care brushing the syrup over the cake and be sure to use it all up.**

- **Brush the cake with the syrup while the cake is hot to ensure it soaks in.**

- **I boil the marmalade in a bowl in the microwave but a pan is fine as long as the marmalade is boiling and lump free so it sticks to the cake.**

- **This cake tastes amazing the day after making as the orange flavour really comes through.**

Orange Polenta Cake

Makes one 20cm cake

Cake
80g polenta
1 tsp baking powder
pinch salt
160g ground almonds
160g unsalted butter
160g caster sugar
zest of 4 large oranges
2 medium eggs
Glaze
50g orange juice
40g caster sugar
Icing sugar to finish

1.   Preheat the oven to 150°C (non fan oven 170°C).
2.   Line a 20cm loose bottomed tin with parchment paper and place aside.
3.   Weigh the almonds, salt, polenta and baking powder in a large bowl.
4.   Stir together with a whisk until well blended then place aside.
5.   Soften the butter and place in the bowl for a stand mixer.
6.   Add the orange zest and caster sugar.
7.   Cream with the whisk attachment for 5-6 minutes until light then scrape down.
8.   Add the eggs one at a time beating each in well.
9.   Remove the bowl from the machine and add the dry ingredients.
10. Fold together with a maris until the mixture is smooth.
11. Scrape into the tin and spread level.
12. Bake for 30-35 minutes until the centre feels slightly firm to the touch.
13. Meanwhile halve the oranges and squeeze the juice through a sieve into a bowl.
14. Weigh 70g of juice into a small pan then add 40g of caster sugar and bring to the boil.
15. Simmer for 1 minute then place aside to cool slightly.
16. When the cake is ready remove from the oven.
17. Leave the cake in the tin and immediately brush the cake all over with all of the syrup.
18. Cool in the tin for 30 minutes then carefully remove the tin but leave on the base.
19. Place into an airtight container and leave to cool for at least 2 hours.
20. Carefully remove the cake from the base and place onto a cake card or plate.
21. To serve dust lightly with icing sugar.

Polenta is used in a lot of Italian desserts and cakes. I first saw a version of a polenta cake when I ate at the River Café in the late 90's during a dinner trip with the lovely Diane Baird who I worked with at All Souls Church in London. This is a cake but in Italy it is served as a dessert or as they would call it Dolci meaning "sweet". This is not a fluffy light cake it has a coarse sticky texture but typical of the cakes found in trendy cafés. I love the orange flavour in this cake from the large amount of zest which gives the cake a gorgeous perfume and the syrup made from the juice adds a lovely sticky orange top. You could use lemons as an alternative just substitute the 4 large oranges for 6 lemons.

Polenta is ground maize so this cake is gluten free so makes an excellent dessert or cake for people with a coeliac condition. As the cake contains no flour it will sink a little in the centre and this is exactly how it should be so don't panic if you think you have a made a mistake during baking. When testing you will see the centre firm up a little it won't spring back like a normal cake so when the centre appears slightly firm to the touch take it out. If you under-bake it don't worry, it's not a major problem the cake will just be a little stickier.

Tim's Tips

- I leave the cake on the base of the cake tin overnight in the airtight container to allow the cake to settle and be less fragile.

- To remove the cake from the tin base place a piece of parchment on top of the cake place a plate or cake card on top then turn over. Remove the base of the tin and the paper then place a plate or cake card on top and flip over to turn the cake the correct way up again.

- Do not try and lift the cake when warm as it's very fragile.

- This cake actually keeps better in the fridge and it's also easier to cut when cold but allow to come to room temperature before serving.

- You only need the juice from about 1-2 of the oranges so drink the rest!

Pear & Ginger Cake

Makes one 20cm cake

Pears
4-6 pears (450g net weight)
35g unsalted butter
35g caster sugar
Cake
100g unsalted butter
(slightly softened)
100g caster sugar
1 tsp vanilla extract
2 medium eggs
150g plain flour
1 tsp baking powder
zest of 1 lemon
1 tsp ground ginger
Topping
25g demerara sugar
½ tsp ground ginger
icing sugar to dust

1. Pre-heat the oven to 160°C (non fan oven 180°C).
2. Line a 20cm loose bottomed tin with parchment paper and place aside.
3. Line a small tray with parchment paper and place into the freezer or fridge.
4. Weigh the flour, ginger and baking powder, sift onto parchment and place aside.
5. Peel and remove the cores from the pears then cut into 2cm chunks.
6. Heat the 35g of butter and 35g of sugar in a pan until bubbling.
7. Add the pears and cook over a high heat until the pears are softened and sticky.
8. Tip the pears onto the cooled tray and place into the fridge or freezer to cool.
9. Place the butter, sugar, vanilla and lemon zest into a stand mixer bowl.
10. Cream with a whisk for 3-4 minutes on medium speed until quite light.
11. Add the eggs one at a time beating each in well.
12. Remove the bowl from the machine and add the dry ingredients.
13. Gently fold together with a maris until smooth and lump free.
14. Add half the pears to the batter and mix in well with a maris.
15. Scrape the cake batter into the tin and spread level.
16. Place the remaining pears evenly over the cake batter.
17. Mix the ½ tsp of ginger with the demerara sugar and sprinkle evenly over the cake.
18. Bake for 40-45 minutes until the sponge springs back.
19. Leave to cool in the tin for 30 minutes.
20. Lift the cake out of the tin and place into an airtight container.
21. When ready to serve slice and dust the cake with icing sugar.

Pears are seldom used in cakes probably because they have a stubborn habit of either being rock hard or very soft and over-ripe. Pears in fact contain an enzyme that ripens a pear rapidly in a short space of time. For this recipe you need pears that are slightly soft but retain a little firmness so judging when that occurs is the only difficult aspect to making this cake. I have always favoured Williams or Comice pears, I find Conference pears a bit woody and not very exciting. There are many excellent varieties available so chose the one you like.

The cooking and chilling of the pears is the most important aspect to success for this cake. I use a large frying pan (free from grease and contamination) as I find this cooks the pears better. Do not pile them into a small pan or the pears will simply boil and not cook out well. You need to cook the pears in very hot butter and sugar so that they release their juice. As they cook the juice evaporates and the pears take on a glassy appearance becoming lovely and sticky. Ensure that the pears are chilled well prior to adding to the cake batter or they all sink to the bottom. I love the warm undertone of ginger with the pears it's a lovely combination that I hope you will love too. A touch of lemon zest in the cake lifts the flavour beautifully.

Tim's Tips

- **Use ripe but still slightly firm pears for the best results.**
- **Place a parchment lined tray in the freezer before cooking the pears.**
- **A teaspoon of ground ginger in the cake gives a lovely warm balance if you love ginger you could add more.**
- **Cook the pears over a high heat shaking the pan to get the best results.**
- **The cake tastes much better and has a softer crumb 24 hours after baking.**

Pecan Blondies

Makes 20 blondies

250g pecans
195g unsalted butter
250g white chocolate pistoles
320g light brown sugar
3 medium eggs
2 tsp vanilla extract
250g plain flour
1 tsp baking powder
½ tsp salt

1. Preheat the oven to 170°C (non fan oven 190°C).
2. Line a 30cm x 20cm brownie tin with parchment paper and place aside.
3. Put the pecans on a tray and bake at for 8-10 minutes until nicely coloured.
4. Place aside to cool then reduce the oven to 160°C (non fan oven 180°C).
5. Weigh the flour, salt and baking powder then sieve onto parchment and place aside.
6. Melt the butter in a bowl in the microwave.
7. Place the eggs and light brown sugar into the bowl for a stand mixer.
8. Using the whisk attachment mix for 3-4 minutes on high speed.
9. Turn the machine off then add all the butter then whisk on medium for 1 minute.
10. Remove the bowl from the machine and add the sifted ingredients.
11. Roughly chop the pecans and add to the bowl with the chocolate.
12. Fold together with a maris until smooth.
13. Scrape into the tin and spread level.
14. Bake for 35-40 minutes then gently press and check with a skewer.
15. There should be a little mixture left on the skewer.
16. Remove from the oven and place aside to cool for at least 2 hours.
17. Remove the blondie from the tin by inverting onto a parchment lined tray.
18. Press the edges of the blondie to flatten the sheet.
19. Place into the fridge to chill for 1 hour.
20. Cut the edges off the blondie and cut the slab into 20 pieces (5 x 4).
21. Store the blondies in an airtight container.

Blondies are the less well known cousin of the American classic chocolate brownie. They get their name from the colour of the finished cake. Using white chocolate as opposed to the dark in brownies so that the finished cake ends up a light golden honey colour. I like to use nuts in my blondies and for this version I prefer pecans. There is a bit of work in the prep to get the desired result as the pecans must be toasted first to make them crunchy and bring out their flavour.

I worked on this recipe for quite a while to get the desired crust which for me is a necessity for all brownie type cakes. This is achieved by the whisking of the sugar and eggs which creates tiny air bubbles that makes the crust biscuit like when baked. The recipe has a fairly high level of salt and vanilla but this is essential as the recipe contains white chocolate which needs the salt to counteract the sweetness and the vanilla to bring out the full flavour.

Tim's Tips

- **The baking requires good judgement, under-baking makes a wet cake over baking results in a dry crumbly cake.**

- **The pecans can be omitted if you prefer, the baking time would be a few minutes less.**

- **You could add semi-dried fruits like raspberries or blueberries as an alternative or as an addition to the pecans.**

- **Other nuts like macadamias and walnuts work well but toast them first.**

- **If you cannot get hold of white chocolate pistoles (buttons) take a bar and chop into 1/2 cm chunks.**

Pineapple Cake

Makes 9 pieces of cake

Pineapple
320g fresh pineapple (net weight)
40g caster sugar
30g unsalted butter
juice of 1 lime
Cake
100g unsalted butter
(slightly softened)
100g caster sugar
zest of 1 lime
2 medium eggs
140g plain flour
1 tsp baking powder
icing sugar to dust

1. Preheat the oven to 170°C (non fan oven 190°C).
2. Line a 24cm square tin with parchment paper and place aside.
3. Line a small tray with parchment paper and place into the freezer or fridge.
4. Weigh the flour and baking powder together in a bowl.
5. Sift the flour and baking powder onto a separate piece of parchment and place aside.
6. Remove the top and bottom of the pineapple then peel with a serrated knife.
7. Cut the pineapple into four pieces through the centre.
8. Remove the core from each quarter then dice the pineapple into 2 cm cubes.
9. Weigh the butter in the bowl for a stand mixer.
10. Zest the lime on a fine grater then add the zest to the butter in the machine bowl.
11. Cut the lime in half and squeeze the juice into a small bowl then place aside.
12. Melt the 30g of unsalted butter in a large frying pan then add the 40g of sugar.
13. Add the pineapple and cook on high heat tossing the pan to keep the fruit moving.
14. Add the lime juice and continue cooking on high for 3-4 minutes tossing the pan.
15. When the pineapple is slightly brown and sticky remove from the heat.
16. Drain the pineapple through a sieve into a bowl to collect the syrup for glazing later.
17. Place the drained pineapple onto the cooled tray and place into the freezer or fridge.
18. Add the 100g of caster sugar to the butter and lime zest in the stand mixer bowl.
19. Cream with the whisk attachment for 3-4 minutes on medium speed until light.
20. Add the eggs one at a time beating each in well.
21. Remove the bowl from the machine and add the sieved dry ingredients.

22. Gently fold the cake batter together with a maris until smooth.
23. Scrape the cake batter into the tin and spread level.
24. Place the cooked pineapple pieces evenly over the cake batter.
25. Bake for 25-30 minutes until the sponge springs back.
26. Leave the cake to cool in the tin covered with a clean tea towel for 30 minutes.
27. Glaze the top of the cake with the juices in the small bowl.
28. Lift the cake out of the tin on the paper and place into an airtight container.
29. When the cake is cold trim the edges off the cakes and cut into 9 pieces (3 x 3).
30. Lightly dust the cake with icing sugar before serving.

Pineapple Cake is better known in the UK as a hot pudding and normally served upside down and served with custard. The cake itself is very simple, enhanced only by the zest of a lime which lifts the flavour beautifully. The only thing that needs any attention is the pineapple which must be ripe. I like to cut mine into chunks about 2cm in size so the finished cake is not too difficult to cut. The pineapple pieces should not colour too much. The aim is is to cook them until they release their moisture and slightly colour. I like to add the juice of the lime and reduce this a little as the pineapple cooks adding more flavour.

I then pass the pineapple through a sieve to catch all the cooking juices which I use to glaze the cake. The cake could be used as a pudding, just cut larger pieces and warm before serving. I dislike tinned pineapple as I find it just too sweet and lacking in flavour but if you prefer to use tinned pineapple the recipe will work fine.

Tim's Tips

- **To check the ripeness of a pineapple pull a leaf from the top, if it comes away easily the pineapple is ripe.**

- **I place a paper lined tray in the freezer before starting to cook the pineapples as this cools the pineapple pieces very quickly**

- **Pineapples are full of juice if you have one in your fridge rip the stalk off and stand on its end. Then turn over every day to allow the juice to even itself out otherwise one end is juicy and one end is dry.**

Pistachio & Amaretto Cake

Makes one 20cm cake

Cake
150g unsalted butter
150g caster sugar
few drops almond extract
3 medium eggs
100g plain flour
100g peeled pistachio nuts
50g ground almonds
¾ tsp baking powder
1 tsp whole milk
Amaretto Buttercream
1 batch of Italian buttercream (page 77)
few drops almond extract
40g amaretto
green food colouring
120g prepared Bonne Maman apricot jam (page 74)
40g coarsely ground pistachios

1. Preheat the oven to 170°C (non fan oven 190°C).
2. Line two 20cm loose bottomed tins with parchment and place aside.
3. Weigh the flour, baking powder and ground almonds in a bowl.
4. Weigh the pistachio nuts and add to the bowl.
5. Place all the dry ingredients into a food processor and blitz for 1 minute.
6. Tip back into a bowl and place aside.
7. Place the butter, caster sugar and almond extract into the bowl for a stand mixer.
8. Cream with the whisk attachment for 4-5 minutes on medium speed until very light.
9. Beat in the eggs one at a time on medium speed mixing each in well.
10. Remove the bowl from the machine and add the dry ingredients in one go.
11. Fold together carefully with a maris until smooth.
12. Add the milk and fold in until smooth.
13. Place 340g of the batter into each tin and spread level with a spoon.
14. Bake for 25-30 minutes until springy.
15. Leave to cool in the tins for 15 minutes covered with a clean tea towel.
16. Remove from the tins and place into an airtight container.

17. Make the buttercream (page 77) then whisk in the extract and amaretto to taste.
18. Colour the buttercream to your desired shade.
19. Place the two sponges onto the table.
20. Spread one sponge crust side up with the jam up to the edge of the sponge.
21. Place one third of the buttercream on top of the jam.
22. Spread the buttercream evenly over the sponge just over the edge of the sponge.
23. Place the other sponge on top crust side down and lightly press together.
24. Spread a thin even layer of buttercream on the side of the cake.
25. Spread or pipe the remaining buttercream on the top of the cake.
26. Crush or blitz the pistachios and sprinkle over the top edge of the cake.
27. Place into the fridge to chill for one hour.

Pistachios are lovely, I adore their subtle almond flavour. They go brilliantly in ice creams and confectionery but also in cakes. I like to pair pistachio with amaretto liquor which despite its almond flavour is actually made from the stones of apricots or peaches and sometimes almonds.

I blitz the pistachios in the food processor with the flour, almonds and baking powder to a coarse texture. This process removes the need for sieving the dry ingredients and stops the oil coming out of the nuts as they blend. The cake is quite rich so I add a layer of apricot jam to add a fruity note. I like to pipe a neat spiral on top of my cake but if this is too fussy for you just spread an even layer of the butter cream on the top and sides.

Tim's Tips

- **Second grade pistachios are peeled but with some skin attached. These are perfect for this cake and a fair bit cheaper.**

- **If you can get super green top grade pistachios use them for the decoration.**

- **All buttercream cakes benefit from about 30 minutes chilling to set the buttercream but serve the cake at room temperature.**

- **I like to pipe my buttercream on the top using a small plain 4mm piping tube and a cake turntable.**

Plum Crumble Cake

Makes 15 pieces of cake

Crumble Mix
80g plain flour
50g unsalted butter
(cold and diced quite small)
40g granulated sugar
Plums
400g plums (net weight)
50g caster sugar
40g unsalted butter
pinch of cinnamon
good pinch lemon zest
squeeze lemon juice
Cake
150g softened unsalted butter
150g caster sugar
1 tsp vanilla extract
3 medium eggs
190g plain flour
1 tsp baking powder

1.   Preheat the oven to 170°C (non fan oven 190°C).
2.   Line a 30cm x 20cm brownie tin with parchment paper and place aside.
3.   Line a small tray with parchment paper and place into the freezer or fridge.
4.   Cut the plums in half and remove the stones then cut each half into four.
5.   Melt the butter and sugar then cook the plums quickly over high heat.
6.   Cook the plums until they release their juice, reduce then become sticky.
7.   When the plums are softened remove from the heat.
8.   Add the cinnamon, lemon zest and lemon juice and stir together well.
9.   Pour the plums juice and all onto the tray and place back in the freezer or fridge.
10. For the crumble place the flour into a bowl for a stand mixer.
11. Add the cold butter and mix until the mixture resembles breadcrumbs.
12. Add the granulated sugar and mix in very quickly then place into a bowl.
13. Weigh the flour and baking powder then sift onto a separate piece of parchment.
14. Place the butter, sugar and vanilla into the same machine bowl used for the crumble.
15. Cream with the whisk attachment for 3-4 minutes on medium speed until quite light.
16. Add the eggs one at a time beating in each well then remove the bowl from the machine.

17. Add the dry ingredients and mix in carefully with a maris.
18. Add the cooled plums and any juice that is on the tray.
19. Fold gently together with a maris then scrape the batter into the tin.
20. Spread the batter level then scatter the crumble mix evenly over the top.
21. Bake for 40-45 minutes.
22. When the cake springs back and a skewer comes out clean remove from the oven.
23. Place aside to cool for 30 minutes then lift the cake out with the paper.
24. Place into an airtight box until the next day.
25. To serve trim off the edges and cut the cake into 18 pieces (6 x 3).

Plums are often used in crumbles and pies but less often in cakes. I love their slightly tart flavour and the texture of them once cooked in cakes. This version has the addition of a crunchy crumble topping which adds another texture. Use whatever plums are available but I particularly like red plums.

I cook the plums rapidly over high heat with sugar and butter to extract some of the moisture before baking. If you use raw plums they release too much liquid during the baking process which makes the cake soggy. The crumble is added raw but bakes beautifully on the top adding a nice texture. The cake is lifted by a touch of lemon and cinnamon added to the plums. Other fruits can be used, I like apricots or peaches.

Tim's Tips

- I like to cut the plums into smallish chunks. If the plum pieces are too big it's difficult to cut the cake.

- I always place a paper lined tray into the freezer for the cooked plums so that they cool down very quickly.

- Add the plums to the cake batter when cold or they will sink to the bottom.

- I always add the thickened juice from the tray with the cooked plums to the batter as it adds a lovely flavour and colour.

Raspberry Cake

Makes 12 portions of cake

Raspberry Sponges
250g plain flour
1¾ tsp baking powder
250g unsalted butter
250g caster sugar
4 medium eggs
1 tsp raspberry flavour
red food colouring
3 tsp whole milk
Jam
100g prepared raspberry jam (page 74)
Raspberry Buttercream
1 batch Italian buttercream (page 77)
red food colouring
raspberry flavouring to taste
about 200g fresh raspberries to decorate

1. Preheat the oven to 170°C (non fan oven 190°C).
2. Line 3 x 20cm loose bottomed tins with parchment and place aside.
3. Weigh the flour and baking powder then sieve onto parchment and place aside.
4. Place the butter and caster sugar into the bowl for a stand mixer.
5. Add the raspberry flavour and a few drops of red colour.
6. Using the whisk attachment cream the butter, sugar and flavouring.
7. Whisk on medium speed for 4-5 minutes until light.
8. Add the eggs on medium speed one at a time mixing each in well.
9. Remove the bowl from the machine and add the sifted dry ingredients.
10. Fold in carefully with a maris until smooth and free from lumps.
11. Add the milk and fold in carefully with a maris.
12. Weigh 310g of cake batter into each of the tins and spread level.
13. Bake for 20-25 minutes or until the sponges spring back.
14. Leave to cool in the tins for 20 minutes covered with a clean tea towels.
15. Remove the sponges from the tins and place into an airtight container.
16. Make the buttercream as per the recipe (page 77).
17. Add raspberry flavour to taste and mix in well.
18. Add a few drops of red food colour and mix in well.

19. Place one sponge onto a plate or cake card.
20. Spread half the jam thinly up to the edges of the sponge.
21. Place the second sponge on top and gently press down the cake to level.
22. Repeat with the jam then press the last sponge on top.
23. Press the sponges down lightly to flatten.
24. Cover the top and sides with the half of the buttercream.
25. Decorate the top with the remaining buttercream and fresh raspberries.

Raspberries are many people's favourite fruit so I wanted to create a raspberry layer cake that would look amazing under a glass dome in a café. The sponge is simple to make and ideal for layered cakes. The cake has a few steps but the end result is both pretty and bursting with raspberry flavour that's well worth the effort. I use jam with the buttercream as it breaks up the pink layers and adds a much needed sharper element to the neutral sponge. I use Bonne Maman jams as I love the fresh fruity flavour. The fresh raspberries are very pretty for the presentation and essential to cut through the sweet cake so use the best ones you can find.

Tim's Tips

- **Do not over bake the sponges or your cake will be dry.**

- **Use the prepared jam (page 74) as jam straight from the jar is too soft.**

- **I usually prepare the entire jar of jam and keep it ready to use in the fridge.**

- **The buttercream is very smooth and not too sweet. It does involve a bit of work but the result is excellent.**

- **This cake is best stored in the fridge but allow to come to room temperature for an hour before serving.**

Rhubarb & Vanilla Cake

Makes 12 pieces

Vanilla Sugar
seeds from 2 vanilla pods
200g caster sugar
Rhubarb
300g pink forced rhubarb
Cake
110g softened unsalted butter
110g vanilla sugar (above)
1 tsp vanilla extract
2 medium eggs
120g plain flour
1 tsp baking powder
50g ground almonds
1 tsp whole milk

1. Preheat the oven to 170°C (non fan oven 190°C).
2. Line a small tray with parchment paper and place into the freezer or fridge.
3. Cut the vanilla pods in half lengthways and scrape the seeds out.
4. Add the vanilla seeds to the 200g of sugar then blitz together in a food processor.
5. Trim the ends off the rhubarb then cut the rhubarb into 1cm chunks.
6. Wash the rhubarb then place into a sieve and shake off the excess water.
7. Place the rhubarb into a large stainless steel pan.
8. Add 70g of the vanilla sugar and the 2 scraped out vanilla pods.
9. Warm the pan until the rhubarb and sugar come to the boil.
10. Immediately remove from the heat and place a lid onto the pan.
11. Leave to gently finish cooking for 5 minutes off the heat in the pan with the lid on.
12. Line a 24cm square tin with parchment and place aside.
13. Weigh the flour and baking powder in a bowl.
14. Sift onto a separate piece of parchment add the ground almonds and place aside.
15. Strain the rhubarb through a sieve into a small pan to catch the juices.
16. Place the rhubarb chunks onto the chilled tray and return to the freezer or fridge.
17. Place the butter, 110g of the vanilla sugar and extract into the bowl for a stand mixer.
18. Using the whisk attachment cream the butter, sugar and extract on medium speed.
19. Cream for 4-5 minutes then add the eggs one at a time mixing in each well.
20. Remove the bowl from the machine then scrape down.
21. Add the sifted dry ingredients and ground almonds.
22. Mix together well with a maris until smooth and lump free.
23. Add the milk and mix in well until smooth.

24. Scrape the cake batter into the tin and spread level.
25. Scatter the chilled rhubarb pieces evenly over the cake batter.
26. Press the rhubarb pieces into the cake to flatten the top.
27. Bake for 25-30 minutes until the cake springs back.
28. Reduce the rhubarb liquid to a nice syrupy consistency (keep an eye on it).
29. When the cake is baked remove from the oven.
30. Brush the cake immediately with the reduced rhubarb syrup.
31. Leave to cool for 30 minutes in the tin.
32. Remove the cake from the tin using the paper to lift it out.
33. Place into an airtight box and leave until completely cold.
34. Remove the edges of the cake then cut into 9 pieces (3 x 3).
35. When serving sprinkle the pieces with the left over vanilla sugar.

Rhubarb as my tutor and pastry hero Professor John Huber once said is a much underused ingredient. I have to say I use it in lots of dishes. I love the forced version from Yorkshire when it's in season. You can get a reasonable substitute from Holland when the Yorkshire one is not available. The Yorkshire variety is available around late December to March-April. I use some ground almonds in this recipe which helps keep the cake moist. If nuts are an issue you can swap the almonds with the same weight of flour but the cake will be a little dryer. Remember to sprinkle the remaining vanilla sugar over the cake only when you serve it as it will dissolve after about 30 minutes.

Tim's Tips

- **Non forced rhubarb is ok just peel it first as it tends to be a bit woody.**

- **Don't overcook the rhubarb it needs a bit of firmness prior to baking.**

- **Do not discard the vanilla pods wash them out, dry them then reuse or place into a pot of caster sugar to make your own vanilla sugar.**

- **Be careful not to burn the cooking liquid, reduce it to a nice sticky syrup to brush the cake top which adds a lovely flavour.**

- **I cut the cake into 9 pieces but cut it to your own preference.**

Salted Caramel Cake

Makes one 20cm cake

Cake
240g plain flour
1¾ tsp baking powder
240g unsalted butter
240g caster sugar
4 medium eggs
½ tsp vanilla extract
1 tbsp whole milk

Salted Caramel
250g caster sugar
20g glucose
250g whipping cream (warm)
100g unsalted butter
1 tsp sea salt (finely ground)

Buttercream
200g unsalted butter (softened slightly)
½ tsp sea salt (finely ground)
350g of the caramel (above)

Topping
130g of the salted caramel
Pistachios & gold leaf (optional)

1. Make the salted caramel first, place a large pan onto the stove to get hot.
2. Gradually add the 250g of caster sugar and gently caramelise to an amber colour.
3. When all the sugar has caramelised add the 100g of butter and stir in until smooth.
4. Place the pan aside then warm the cream in a bowl in the microwave to about 40°C.
5. Gradually add the cream to the caramel and whisk together until smooth.
6. Add the salt and mix in until the mixture is smooth scrape into a dish and chill.
7. Preheat the oven to 170°C (non fan oven 190°C).
8. Line three 20cm loose bottomed tins with parchment and place aside.
9. Weigh the flour and baking powder in a bowl.
10. Sift onto a separate piece of parchment paper and place aside.
11. Place the butter, sugar and vanilla into the bowl for a stand mixer.
12. Cream with the whisk attachment for 5-6 minutes on medium speed until very light.
13. Add the eggs one at a time and beat each one in well.
14. Remove the bowl from the machine and add the sifted dry ingredients.
15. Fold in the dry ingredients carefully with a maris until smooth.
16. Add the milk and mix together carefully with a maris until smooth and lump free.

17. Weigh 310g of cake batter into each tin and spread level with the back of a spoon.
18. Bake for 22-25 minutes or until springy.
19. Leave to cool in the tins for 15 minutes covered with clean tea towels.
20. Remove the sponges from the tins and place into airtight containers.
21. Leave the sponges to cool completely while you make the buttercream.
22. Place 130g of the caramel for the topping in a bowl and place in the fridge.
23. For the buttercream place the 200g of unsalted butter in a stand mixer bowl.
24. Add the salt and a quarter of the caramel base and whisk in on medium speed.
25. Whisk again on medium gradually adding the remaining caramel.
26. Whisk until very light and taste to see if more salt is required.
27. Place a sponge on the table and place about 20% of the buttercream on top.
28. Spread evenly to the sides and repeat with the other two sponges.
29. Cover the top and sides with the remaining buttercream as neatly as you can.
30. Place the cake into the fridge to chill for at least one hour.
31. Take the remaining caramel out of the fridge to warm up slightly for 20 minutes.
32. When the cake is cold spread the caramel over the top of the cake.
33. Decorate with nuts or gold leaf as desired.

Salted Caramel is one of my favourite flavours in everything from hand-made chocolates to ice cream. I spent a lot of time getting this recipe right trying to ensure it's packed with flavour whilst not being too sweet. Make the caramel first then reserve 130g for the top and use the rest for the buttercream. I like to use a comb scraper to mark the sides but as long as you get some caramel buttercream between the layers with a nice even coat on the top and sides it really doesn't matter.

Take care to chill the cake completely before adding the reserved caramel topping. If you make this right it should stick to the top but remain soft. The level of salt is entirely personal I tend to use slightly more than the recipe suggests here but flavour the caramel to your tastes. There is a method on how to make a dry caramel on page 76. Take the caramel out of the fridge for 20 minutes prior to spreading on the cold cake.

Tim's Tips

- **I usually make the sponges the day before and leave in an airtight box.**
- **If you have one use a turntable to coat the cake with the buttercream.**
- **I use a scraper to makes the sides flat before using a comb scraper.**
- **I dip a serrated knife in very hot water to ensure clean slices of cake.**
- **Store in the fridge but allow to come to room temperature to serve.**
- **Add the glucose with the last batch of sugar.**

Strawberries & Cream Cake

Makes one 10 portion cake

Cake
235g plain flour
2 tsp baking powder
160g unsalted butter (softened)
5g glycerine
1 tsp vanilla extract
½ tsp strawberry flavour
red food colouring
4 medium eggs
160g caster sugar
2½ tsp whole milk

Vanilla Buttercream
1 batch of Italian buttercream (page 77)
seeds of 1 vanilla pod & ½ tsp vanilla extract
300g fresh strawberries
70g prepared strawberry jam (page 74)

Decorations
finely blitzed pistachios (optional)

1. Preheat the oven to 170°C (non fan oven 190°C).
2. Line 2 x 20cm loose bottomed tins with parchment paper.
3. Sift the flour and baking powder into the bowl for a stand mixer.
4. Add the butter and combine slowly with the beater to form a paste.
5. Add the glycerine and beat on medium speed for 4-5 minutes.
6. Meanwhile place the eggs into a bowl.
7. Using a hand held electric mixer whisk on high speed for 30 seconds.
8. Gradually add the sugar and whisk until pale and quite thick.
9. Scrape a quarter of the mixture into the bowl with the flour and butter.
10. Beat in well until smooth then add the remaining sugar and egg in 3 additions.
11. Remove from the machine and mix together with a maris until smooth.
12. Add the milk and fold in with a maris.
13. Weigh 380g of mixture into two separate bowls.
14. Colour one bowl pink then add the strawberry flavour and fold together.
15. Add the vanilla extract to the other bowl and fold in.
16. Place one batter into each tin and spread level with a dessert spoon.
17. Bake for 15-18 minutes until the sponges spring back.
18. Leave to cool in the tin covered with clean towel towels for 10 minutes.

19. Remove the sponges and transfer into an airtight container to cool completely.
20. Place the two sponges onto the table and level if necessary.
21. Spread the vanilla sponge with the strawberry jam.
22. Place one third of the buttercream on top of the jam.
23. Spread level to the edge then place the other sponge on top and lightly press.
24. Spread a thin layer of buttercream over the top and sides of the cake.
25. Mark the top of the cake into 10 even portions.
26. Pipe buttercream starting from the edge to the centre of the cake on each portion.
27. Pick out 3 strawberries for the centre then slice the remaining strawberries.
28. Arrange the sliced strawberries neatly on the portions of the cake.
29. If using add blitzed pistachios on the top and around the base of the cake.
30. Cut the reserved strawberries in half and place in the centre of the cake neatly.
31. Dust the cake with a little icing sugar to help glaze the fruit.

Strawberries & Cream

Strawberries & Cream are the taste of summer and I wanted to capture that in a recipe. The cake consists of two layers of sponge one vanilla flavoured and one strawberry flavoured. I like to use a layer of strawberry jam and a smooth rich vanilla buttercream finished off with beautiful fresh strawberries. I usually make the buttercream while the cake is baking then leave in the fridge to firm up a little.

My biggest gripe with strawberry cakes is that there are so many strawberries piled on top the cakes are impossible to portion and cut. I mark the cake first pipe the border and place the best strawberries onto the portions making cutting into even slices simple. I adore Kent strawberries which are usually best around June and July.

Tim's Tips

- **Use the very best strawberries you can find and try to avoid buying strawberries with white shoulders which is a sign of forced growing.**

- **The cake should be stored in the fridge but make sure you take it out for about 30 minutes to bring to room temperature before serving.**

- **Wash out and dry the vanilla pod and keep for other uses I like to keep mine in a jar of sugar to make vanilla sugar.**

Sultana Cake

Makes one 20cm cake

230g Whitworths Sunshine Sultanas
170g plain flour
1¾ tsp baking powder
100g unsalted butter
100g golden caster sugar
10g golden syrup
2 medium eggs
35g whole milk
25g demerara sugar

1. Pre-heat the oven to 150°C (non fan oven 170°C).
2. Line 1 x 20cm spring form tin with parchment paper and place aside.
3. Weigh the sultanas in a bowl and place to one side.
4. Weigh the flour and baking powder then sift onto parchment then place aside.
5. Add 1 heaped dessert spoon of the dry ingredients to the sultanas.
6. Mix together until the sultanas are well coated in the dry ingredients.
7. Place the butter, golden syrup and golden caster sugar in a stand mixer bowl.
8. Using the beater attachment cream on medium speed for 4-5 minutes.
9. Add the eggs one at a time beating each in well.
10. Remove the bowl from the machine and scrape down.
11. Place the bowl back onto the machine and add the dry ingredients.
12. Mix slowly until smooth then beat on medium speed for 2 minutes.
13. Add the sultanas and mix for 30 seconds until combined.
14. Add the milk and mix in slowly with a maris until smooth.
15. Place the batter into the tin and spread level with the back of a spoon.
16. Sprinkle the cake evenly with the demerara sugar.
17. Place a pan in the base of the oven and add a little water.
18. Bake for 50-55 minutes until springy and a skewer comes out clean.
19. Leave to cool in the tin for 20 minutes.
20. Remove from the tin and place into an airtight container.

Sultana cake is my tribute to the Mr Kipling cake Manor House, I love the simplicity of this cake with its crumbly texture and moist fruit. The only improvement I have given it is that I use all butter which gives the cake a bit of richness and luxury that the original does not have. I use golden caster sugar and a little bit of golden syrup to give the slightly caramelised flavour that the original has. There is a lot of debate about why fruit falls in a cake and mostly this is because the cake batter is not strong enough to hold the fruit up. To counteract this the batter needs to be beaten slightly longer until it tightens up a little to strengthen the gluten in the batter.

Also be aware that the Whitworths sultanas that I use are lightly coated in oil to retain their softness which tend to slip through the cake mixture as it warms up in the oven so as a precaution I roll these in some of the dry ingredients before adding to the cake batter. This is a lightly fruited cake so ideal for people who don't like overly heavy wedding type fruit cakes. The demerara sugar on top gives a lovely authentic crunchy top.

Tim's Tips

- I use Whitworth's Sunshine Sultanas if you can't get these soak sultanas in boiled water for 10 minutes then drain and dry on a clean tea towel.

- The beating helps strengthen the batter which helps the texture and keeps the fruit from sinking, 2 minutes is just long enough don't overdo this or your cake will be a little tough.

- Do coat the fruit in some of the dry mixture this ensures that the fruit will be evenly distributed throughout the cake and not sink.

- As the cake is in the oven for nearly an hour a little pan of water helps the crust from becoming too dry.

The Best Chocolate Brownie In The World

Makes 20 brownies

275g unsalted butter
275g 70% dark chocolate
(I use St Domingue)
500g dark brown sugar
4 medium eggs
160g plain flour
2 tsp baking powder
pinch of salt

1. Preheat the oven to 160°C (180°C).
2. Line a 30cm x 20cm brownie tin with parchment and place aside.
3. Weigh the flour, baking powder and salt into a bowl.
4. Sieve these dry ingredients onto a separate piece of parchment and place aside.
5. Melt the butter in a plastic bowl on medium in the microwave.
6. Add the chocolate and microwave again in 30 second bursts on medium.
7. Heat until the chocolate has almost melted then remove and stir together.
8. Mix until completely smooth and lump free then place aside.
9. Place the brown sugar and eggs into the bowl for a stand mixer.
10. Mix with the beater attachment on medium for 4 minutes until light and well risen.
11. Add the melted butter/chocolate and mix in slowly until blended.
12. Add the sifted dry ingredients to the bowl and mix slowly until well blended.
13. Remove from the machine mix with a maris to ensure there are no lumps of flour.
14. Scrape the mixture into the tin and spread level.
15. Bake for 30 minutes then check the oven turn the tray around if required.
16. Bake for a further 15 minutes, check again.
17. Bake for another 5-10 minutes depending on your preference
    (Approximate total baking time 50-60 minutes).
18. Cool for 30 minutes then turn out onto a parchment lined tray.
19. Carefully press the edges of the brownie to flatten.
20. Cling film the tray leave at room temperature for at least 2 hours.
21. Remove the edges of the brownie.
22. Cut the brownie into 20 pieces (5 x 4).
23. Place into an airtight box or the fridge but eat at room temperature.

The best Chocolate Brownie in the world is a very bold claim indeed. It always reminds me of my friend Jennifer Earle the renowned chocolate expert. I had posted this statement on Twitter as at the time I was running a chocolate outlet selling my hand-made chocolates. I had exchanged messages with Jen via social media and so when this charming lady walked into the shop and asked for the best chocolate brownie in the world I knew exactly who she was. We have been friends ever since.

To me a brownie must be intensely chocolatey and gooey in the middle but not too sweet. The crust top and bottom must also be dry so that you can pick it up and bite into it without getting sticky fingers. It's essential to use at least 70% chocolate (I use a single origin St Domingue 70%) and also dark brown sugar. If you look at any brownie recipe the sugar is the highest ingredient in the recipe which with the under baking creates the gooey centre. The problem is of course that caster sugar is very sweet so by using brown sugar you get the gooey texture without the overbearing sweetness.

The crust is formed by beating the brown sugar and eggs with a beater (not the whisk attachment). By doing this the aeration takes longer and the air bubbles formed by this process are very small and when the other ingredients are mixed these tiny air bubbles are light so they rise to the top of the batter and form a lovely biscuit like crust. I use a brownie tin that I bought in New York in 1995 which is heavy and helps bake the bottom of the brownie nice and dry. I have found 50-55 minutes is perfect depending on how gooey you personally like your brownies.

Tim's Tips

- **Use really good chocolate, I like 70% St Domingue or 75% Tanzanian but good quality 70% off the shelf is ok.**

- **The baking powder lifts the brownie slightly giving an excellent texture.**

- **Don't forget the pinch of salt this helps to bring out the chocolate flavour.**

- **Experiment with the timing until you get the brownie how you like it.**

- **Try to find a tin 30cm x 20cm if you use a smaller tin the brownie will be too dense and be far too wet in the centre.**

Victoria Sandwich

Makes one 10 portion cake

Cake
200g unsalted butter
200g caster sugar
1 tsp vanilla extract
4 medium eggs
200g plain flour
30g cornflour
2 tsp baking powder
Buttercream
60g unsalted butter
75g icing sugar
½ tsp vanilla extract
120g prepared Bonne Mama raspberry jam (page 74)
Caster Sugar to dust

1. Preheat the oven to 170°C (non fan oven 190°C).
2. Grease two 20cm loose bottomed tins with very soft butter.
3. Place a circle of parchment paper on the bottom of the tins (do not line the sides).
4. Weigh the flour, baking powder and cornflour in a bowl.
5. Sift the dry ingredients onto a separate piece of parchment and place aside.
6. Place the butter, vanilla and sugar together in a bowl for a stand mixer.
7. Cream with the whisk attachment on medium speed for 3-4 minutes.
8. Scrape down then add the eggs one at a time whisking in each well.
9. Remove the bowl from the machine and scrape the bowl down.
10. Add the dry ingredients and fold in very carefully with a maris.
11. Place 300g of mixture into each tin and spread level (add any extra batter evenly).
12. Bake for 22-25 minutes until springy and golden brown.
13. Remove from the oven and leave to cool in the tin for 5 minutes.
14. Remove the sponges from the tins leaving the paper on the bases.
15. Place into an airtight box to cool completely (do not stack).
16. To make the buttercream place the butter and icing sugar in a bowl.
17. Add the vanilla and whisk with the hand held electric whisk until light.
18. Place both sponges onto the table top crust sides down on the counter.
19. Spread the jam onto one sponge right to the edge.
20. Spread the buttercream evenly onto the other sponge to the edge and place on top.
21. Place the cake onto a cake card or plate and press lightly together.

22. Place the cake into the fridge for 30 minutes to firm up.
23. Cut into portions with a knife dipped in hot water and wiped with a cloth.
24. Dust the cake with caster sugar through a tea strainer.
25. Place into an airtight box and allow to come fully to room temperature.

Victoria Sandwich

Victoria Sandwich is of course a classic cake named after Queen Victoria although the exact date is unknown. The classic Victoria sandwich is an equal measure cake using the classic creaming method and traditionally only sandwiched together with raspberry jam. My version has a simple vanilla buttercream as an alternative to the Italian buttercream added as I think this goes perfectly with the jam. Raspberry jam however good a quality used straight from the jar is too soft when the slices are cut, also I hate seeds left in jam so I always use a prepared one (page 74).

For my sponges I add a little cornflour and use slightly more flour than equal measures as I find I get a super light cake that never collapses. Place the cakes into an airtight box overnight you will be astonished at the resulting light moist sponge, trust me on this and try it.

Tim's Tips

- Use butter that is cool but not too hard, creaming the cool butter incorporates a lot of air and makes for a light sponge.

- Don't be tempted to soften the butter too much as oily butter does not incorporate air well and makes for a heavy close textured cake.

- To grease the tins I use softened butter and brush the sides with a thin even coating and just a dab to hold the circle of paper in place.

- By not lining the sides of the tin with paper you will get a nice flat outside edge to your cake.

- To get a perfect cut I place the cake into the fridge for 30 minutes to firm up the buttercream then cut into 10 portions dipping the blade in hot water. Do not store the cake in the fridge after setting or the cake goes hard.

- I dust the top of the cake with caster sugar through a tea strainer after cutting which makes for very neat slices of cake.

Marzipan

Makes about 250g of marzipan

135g ground almonds
105g icing sugar
6 tsp cold water
½ tsp almond extract

1. Weigh the sugar and ground almonds together.
2. Place into a food processor and blitz for about 1 minute until fine.
3. Add the water and almond extract and blend until a paste is formed.
4. Scrape the paste onto the table.
5. Carefully knead the paste until smooth and comes together.
6. Place the marzipan into a freezer bag or wrap in cling film.
7. Leave for at least an hour to firm up.
8. Place into a plastic bag and store in an airtight container.

Marzipan is an ingredient I have always loved either wrapped around my favourite cake Battenberg or moulded into beautiful fruits for almond petit fours. I usually make my own marzipan as I like my marzipan less sweet than the versions available in the supermarket. This version dries out a little firmer than the supermarket brands which is what I am looking for to wrap around my battenberg cake.

I use about 50% almonds so my version is more like an almond paste. Marzipan is very quick and easy to make, this recipe takes only a few minutes to make in a food processor and a couple hours to firm up. Once you make your own you may never buy the shop bought one again.

Tim's Tips

- **The blending of the almonds and icing sugar makes the marzipan smooth.**

- **It's essential to blitz the icing sugar with the almonds to prevent them becoming oily which would make the marzipan greasy.**

- **Keep the marzipan in a plastic bag at all times to prevent drying out.**

- **I use Nielsen Massey almond extract, you may need to adjust how much almond extract you use depending on the strength, use caution.**

Jams
Preparation for one jar of jam

1 jar Bonne Maman conserve
(apricot, raspberry or strawberry)

1. Scrape the entire jar of conserve into a plastic bowl (keep the jar).
2. Heat in the microwave until fairly hot.
3. Place a sieve over a small pan and press the conserve through the sieve.
4. Press to remove the seeds and large chunks of fruit pieces.
5. Place the pan onto the heat and bring gently up to the boil.
6. Simmer gently for 3 minutes stirring occasionally.
7. Remove from the heat and scrape the reduced conserve into a bowl.
8. Leave the maris in the bowl and stir occasionally until tepid.
9. When tepid scrape the conserve back into the jar and place into the fridge.

Bonne Maman Conserves are my go to choice mostly for their glorious fruit flavour. I use their raspberry, strawberry and apricot conserves as the fruit content is so high. This is important because when you reduce the conserve it makes the flavour sweeter so if you start with a sweet jam it becomes unbearably sweet. The reason I prepare my conserves is that jam straight from the jar is far too soft and runs out of cakes making them messy. Also I personally dislike seeds in jam and want them removed. It doesn't take long to prepare the jam and I think the end result is worth it. I find it best to prep the whole jar then it's in your fridge ready to go when you need it.

Tim's Tips

- **Other preserves are available but check the jar, you need a fruit content higher than the sugar content or the prepared jam will be too sweet.**

- **Once prepared keep the jam in the fridge, it will keep for at least 2 weeks.**

- **I find simmering on a medium heat for 3 minutes to reduce is just right.**

Chocolate Hazelnut Spread

Makes about 400g

250g praline paste 1:1 (50% sugar)
20g milk chocolate
75g 70% dark chocolate
pinch of salt
30g sunflower oil

1. Place the milk and dark chocolate in a plastic bowl.
2. Heat in the microwave in 30 second bursts on medium until melted and lump free.
3. Add the praline paste and sunflower oil and whisk in.
4. Add the salt and whisk in.
5. Scrape into a sterilised 1lb jar.
6. Place into the fridge for 3 hours to set then store at room temperature.
7. Once opened it keeps for 2 weeks (or 5 minutes if you are a chocoholic).

Chocolate and Hazelnut is one of my favourite flavour combinations particularly in a spread like Nutella. I know a lot of people have an issue with products containing palm oil, I do too so I created this alternative. This recipe is incredibly easy and tastes amazing but it does require you to purchase a tub of hazelnut praline paste.

Hazelnut praline paste is 50% sugar and 50% toasted hazelnuts ground together. Commercial praline pastes are smooth delicious and relatively inexpensive for what they are. I buy mine online and many varieties are available look for a 50:50 paste the brand made by Callebaut is particularly good. Make sure that you sterilise the jar before using by rinsing out with boiled water and then drying in a low oven on a wire rack.

Tim's Tips

- Give the praline paste a really good stir with a spoon before you use it as the oil tends to float to the top.

- I prefer the balance of flavour using a 70% dark chocolate but if you prefer a sweeter flavour use a 55% dark chocolate.

Dry Caramel Technique

When I was studying under Professor John Huber at Slough College he showed us how to make a dry or direct caramel. He said if you caramelised sugar without any water the caramel flavour was better, we thought it would burn without any water but he just smiled and said let me show you. He placed a pan with nothing in it on the stove over a moderate heat. Then he got a pot of caster sugar and added a spoonful to the pan. The first thing it did was stick to the pan and not move, then it gradually went from granular to a clear syrup then slowly into an amber colour.

As the pan got hotter John added more sugar, a spoon at a time and melted this into the caramel. He then added more sugar equal to the amount of caramel which he assured us the pan could cope with it. After a few minutes he had a pan of amber coloured caramel that wasn't burnt or crystallised. He then said this recipe (as do many with caramel) required a little glucose which is always added with the last batch of sugar. The glucose bubbled then melted into the caramel. The thing he also stressed was that you should not stir the pan until you added cream or butter in case it crystalised. The recipe he made did require cream and butter which he added. He explained that as soon as you added cream and/or butter the sugar would not burn as the moisture prevented this.

As I use a dry caramel for some recipes in this book I thought it a good idea to share this technique. So here below are pictures of how the technique should be used. As with all caramels take great care as sugar burns are particularly painful! I always weigh my glucose on the caster sugar and add to the pan with the last batch of sugar.

Italian Buttercream

Makes about 750g buttercream

200g caster sugar
60g water
3 medium eggs
300g unsalted butter (cool)
flavour & colour as desired

1. Cut the butter into 2cm chunks and place aside.
2. Place the sugar and water in a small saucepan and bring to the boil.
3. Cook this sugar syrup until it reaches 120°C (do not stir).
4. Place the eggs in the bowl for a stand mixer and whisk on high speed.
5. Wash down the sides of the syrup as it boils with a brush and water.
6. Once the sugar syrup reaches 120°C remove from the heat.
7. Turn the mixer off and take the pan to the mixer.
8. Pour half of the syrup onto the eggs avoiding the sides.
9. Immediately turn the machine onto top speed.
10. Place the pan back onto the heat on low to keep fluid.
11. Whisk for 20 seconds then turn off again pour on the rest of the syrup.
12. Turn the machine on top speed and whisk until cool for 3-4 minutes.
13. Add the butter, a piece at a time, beating on a medium-high speed.
14. Keep beating until all of the butter is incorporated and is smooth.
15. Add flavours colours at this point and whisk in.
16. Let the buttercream stand for 5-10 minutes to firm up a little in the fridge.

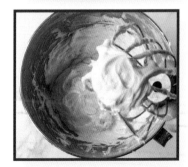

Sugar Batter Cake Making Method

The sugar batter method or the "creaming method" as it's more commonly known is when the sugar and butter are creamed to a light texture, the eggs are then added gradually and mixed in well. The dry ingredients are added next and folded carefully together to make a light smooth cake batter and milk if required is added last and folded in. This is the most common method of making cakes and like all cake methods when executed correctly makes a light delicate cake.

Butter
The butter should be pliable and cool but not fridge cold. I prefer to use the whisk attachment as I think this is easier to lighten the butter and it also incorporates air beautifully. If the butter is too cold you will possibly damage the whisk attachment and it will take quite a long time to cream. If the butter is too warm or semi melted the oil in the butter will be impossible to incorporate air into and you will end up with a tough cake. The other advantage of using the whisk attachment is that the bowl requires less scraping down during the creaming process.

Eggs
The eggs should be as fresh as possible and always be used at room temperature. Crack your eggs into a bowl before you start. It's unlikely but, you may get a bad egg and it's better to lose a few eggs than a batch of cake. It's also easier to remove a random piece of egg shell from a bowl of eggs than to try and find it in a cake batter.

Flour
I always use plain flour and add my own raising agents because I find I get better results. Dry ingredients should be folded into cake batters by hand with a maris on the creaming method to avoid overworking the batter and to ensure a tender product.

Flour and dry ingredients should always be sifted before adding to a cake batter this is to ensure the dry ingredients are well distributed and to remove any foreign bodies like husks of wheat. It is not as some think to incorporate air into your cake this is a myth. I always sift my dry ingredients onto a separate piece of parchment paper and place to the side, this is because when I need it it's good to go. I don't sift directly into the bowl because it's too easy to dip the bottom of the sieve into the butter/sugar/eggs. I find it easier to lift the dry ingredients up on the paper and drop into the bowl in one go.

Method
To make a perfect cake it's vital to understand what role each of the ingredients play and what happens during the cake making process to achieve the best results. For the best results have all the ingredients at the same temperature, cream the butter and sugar until light and then mix in the eggs one at a time until you have a smooth light mixture. Scrape the bowl down to ensure a uniform mixture then add the sifted ingredients and fold together with a maris by hand to a smooth light batter.

If you under mix the sugar and butter you will end up with a heavy cake so cream well. If you over mix the butter and sugar they will become too warm and become oily and again create a heavy cake.

79

If you add cold eggs to the butter and sugar the shock chill of the cold egg forms globules of cold butter suspended in the liquid egg, the very worst thing you can do at this point is to add some of the dry ingredients. Plain flour contains protein ranging from approximately 10-12% if this dry protein touches the wet egg it will hydrate the flour proteins into gluten strands and as the cake mixes these strands get stronger and produce a tough cake.

To avoid this ensure your eggs are room temperature and do not add the dry ingredients until all of the egg has been mixed in. If you mix in your eggs at room temperature gradually you should end up with a smooth mixture. If you slightly curdle the mixture prior to adding the dry ingredients don't worry add all the sifted dry ingredients in one go. The batter should right itself when you carefully fold in the dry ingredients.

As soon as you add any dry ingredients to the butter/sugar/eggs the flour proteins are hydrated into gluten strands and this process cannot be avoided. You can ensure however that they are not over developed by the folding in of the dry ingredients carefully by hand with a maris. If you use the machine it's likely you will over mix the batter. The exceptions are the Sultana Cake and the Genoa Cake where you deliberately want to "slightly" strengthen the batter so that the fruit they contain does not sink.

Flour Batter Cake Making Method

The flour batter method is not very familiar to most people, it has however been around for many years and most bakeries make their slab cakes based on this method. The advantages are a high yield cake with a very fine cake crumb that cuts beautifully and keeps really well. For these reasons this type of sponge is ideal for layer cakes like Battenburg or light to medium fruit cakes. This method is unusual in that you take the four basic ingredients flour, sugar, eggs and butter and mix them together in an entirely different method than seems obvious.

The dry ingredients are sifted into the bowl for a stand mixer with the butter and beaten until very light. The eggs are whisked to a thick sabayon with the sugar and added in four additions to the butter and flour mixture and then mixed briefly until smooth and light. There are several recipes that use this method in this book and this may be unfamiliar to you but do give it a try I think you will be pleasantly surprised with the results.

Method

Sift the dry ingredients into the machine bowl and add slightly softened butter.

Mix briefly until a paste is formed then add flavours and glycerine, and beat until light.

You need to mix the flour and butter to a paste first so that the flour is coated in butter and therefore waterproof before adding any liquids.

Whisk the eggs in a clean bowl until light and frothy and add to the machine bowl in four additions and mix until smooth scraping the bowl down when adding the last of the eggs and sugar.

Scale into your tins, spread level and bake.

Notes

There is no need to sift the dry ingredients onto paper separately as they are mixed with the butter so sift the dry ingredients straight into the machine bowl.

The butter should be slightly soft but cool and not oily.

The bowl and whisk used to aerate the eggs and sugar must be free from grease I usually rinse mine out with boiling water to ensure they are clean.

Most of the aeration in the cake comes from the long beating of the butter and dry ingredients and partially from the air whipped into the eggs and sugar. The resulting cake should be super light and with a fine delicate crumb.

Cakes made on the flour batter method normally have less raising agents than other cakes as the long beating creates aeration by the mechanical process during production.

Equipment

I have always said to my students if you buy the best quality equipment you can afford you will probably only buy it once, so buy the best quality and take care of them and they should last you a lifetime.

These are the essential pieces of equipment that I use in my classes and at home.

Cake Tins

Sizes specified for the recipes are important as baking a cake in the wrong size tin will drastically alter the results and in some cases the recipes won't work at all. Listed here are the cake tins used for this book.

1lb loaf tin (internal measurements 21cm x 11cm)
24cm square tin (internal measurements 21.5cm x 21.5cm x 4cm deep)
20cm round loose bottomed cake tins (flat sided 4cm deep)
I use Alan Silverwood tins which are superb I have 4 of these and use them all the time
24cm spring form tin
20cm spring form tin
30cm x 20cm brownie tin

Baking Sheets

I use several sizes of non-stick baking sheets, I prefer the Vogue brand because they do not bend in the oven. These are great quality and if cared for will last a lifetime.
I use three sizes:
32cm x 22cm
38cm x 28cm
43cm x 31.5cm

Baking Parchment & Cake Liners

I buy my baking parchment in large sheets and cut to fit my trays and tins. If you do a lot of baking this is the best way to purchase it because the paper does not curl up and you can also cut the paper exactly to the size you want and of course it's cheaper.

When I line my tins I use pre-bought circles of parchment paper or I cut my own having drawn a circle with the tin and a pencil. I use strips cut from the sheets for the sides of the tins. I prefer to use cake liners for my 1lb tins, you can cut your own but they do occasionally leak. For brownie tins and square tins I press the parchment paper into the greased tins without cutting so there are no gaps.

Stand Mixer

I use Kitchen Aid mixers at home as I find these superb quality and easy to use, but other excellent machines are made by Kenwood. I use 10 of these in my classes.

Oven Thermometer

These are very useful and are relatively inexpensive. It is a good idea to buy one to check if your oven is at the temperature it says it is so you can adjust as necessary.

Ovens

I use a standard fan oven if you have a non-fan oven set your oven at 20°C higher.

Hand held electric whisk

I use these a fair bit and having both types of machine would be useful especially if you are making the flour batter method because you can make both parts of the mixture at the same time. If you have either a stand mixer or a hand held mixer but not both you can make most of the recipes in this book. The one type of recipe you would find hard to make without a stand mixer would be any cake made on the flour batter method as a beater is required.

Whisks

I use Matfer whisks with sealed handles they last a long time and are excellent quality.

Maris (spatulas)

These are spatulas, the ones I prefer are the spoon ended ones with red handles which denote that they are heatproof, these are perfect for mixing cakes and have the advantage that you can cook with them. I keep my pastry and cooking ones separate.

Scrapers

I use standard scrapers which usually have a rounded edge and 2 straight sides. These are brilliant for scraping out cake batters from mixing bowls, flattening the sides of cakes and for scraping tables clean.

Scales

I use two sets of scales, micro scales that go from 0.01g to 3kg and platform scales with a range of 1g to 10kg. The platform scales are good for this book because you can place a tray on top and place your tins directly onto the trays meaning you can weigh the cake batter directly into the tin which for accuracy is extremely useful.

Bowls

I use high quality orange plastic bowls which are designed for chocolate work being durable and unlikely to crack with use. I buy mine from Keylink but decent quality plastic bowls can be purchased from many outlets or internet shops, buy the best quality ones you can and keep for pastry work only to avoid contamination and smells.

Cake Cards

Many of the cakes need icing or glazing, I use thin cake cards to assemble many of the cakes. These are easy to purchase online I use 20cm, 24cm and 26cm ones.

Measuring Spoons

I use these for small measures as I appreciate not everybody has a micro-scale. A basic set of spoons will suffice I do not use cups in larger sizes just spoons for spices, raising agents, salt, flavours, milk and glycerine.

Sieves

I use all metals sieves that are durable. Plastic sieves are not really strong enough to sieve the jams required for these recipes so invest in a good quality metal one.

Timers

I use timers for all my oven bakes and also for timing mixes too. These are essential pieces of equipment, I have several and often use them at the same time.

Pans
I use all stainless steel pans with metal handles buy good quality ones and they will last a lifetime. I use small ones from 0.5ltr in size up to to 2ltr.

Pastry Brushes
I use only bristle brushes, nylon brushes won't be strong enough and if you use one for brushing pans they will melt. I use wide ones and narrow ones.

Piping Bags
I use disposable piping bags bought in rolls of 100. I don't use nylon or cloth bags because they are unhygienic and harbour smells.

Piping Nozzles
I use several types of nozzles some star shaped and some plain. I have many of these. If you have a basic set of plain and star nozzles that will be fine for the cakes in this book.

Cake Turntable
I use these to evenly spread the sides of cakes that require buttercream and ganache and to pipe the lovely top on the Pistachio Amaretto cake. It is not an essential piece of kit but a good quality metal one that moves nicely certainly makes this task easier.

Probe or Stick Thermometer
I use this to measure the sugar syrup temperature for my Italian buttercream, if you do not have one the recipe advises how to judge the temperature. I think these are invaluable for baking and easy to purchase online so well worth getting one.

Skewer
Very useful tool to determine if the cake is baked correctly, you could use a knife but this may tear your cake.

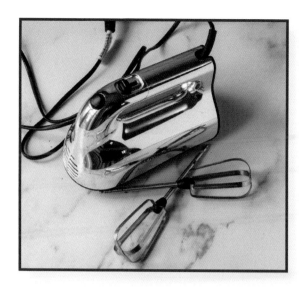

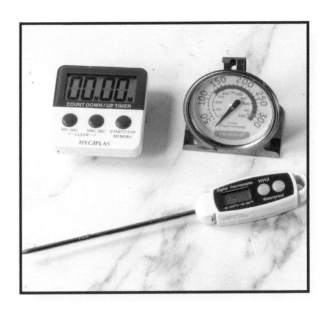

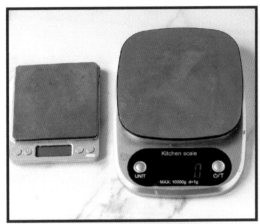

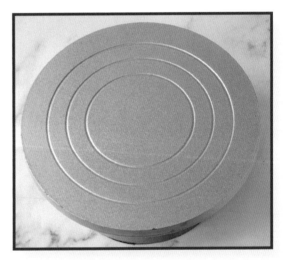

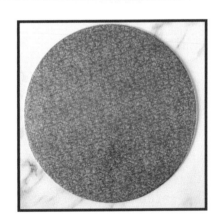

87

Lining Cake Tins

Lining cake tins is an aspect that should not be overlooked as the care taken may affect the quality of the cake when de-moulding especially if it sticks to the tin. You can of course purchase cake liners of many shapes and sizes but whether you use these or not knowing how to line tins with parchment paper is still a good thing to know how to do. I prefer to use liners for my loaf tins as they have no gaps at all and obviously save a lot of time. For lining round tins I mark a circle of parchment paper with the base of the tin with a pencil then cut around this to ensure it is the same size as the interior of the tin. I then cut strips of parchment paper by folding straight lines and running a knife through it.

I prefer to use a grease spray to grease my tins which is purely to hold the paper to the tin. Pre-cut circles of parchment paper are also available and I do occasionally use these too. When I line my brownie tins and square tins for the recipes in this book I cut a piece of parchment about 30% larger than the tin then press the uncut paper into the corners. I prefer to do this as there are no gaps for the batter to run into the tin. For some cakes like the Victoria sandwich I prefer to not line the sides of the tin with paper but grease them lightly with butter. This is to ensure that a nice flat edge is achieved as the sides of the sponge will be in plain view. Most cakes that contain higher levels of sugars or golden syrup need the protection of lining with paper to ensure they release from the tin. Guidance for the lining for each cake is within the individual recipe.

Baking, Storing & Preserving Cakes

When you bake a cake the centre is the last place for the heat to reach so your goal is to ensure the very centre of the cake is cooked. When a cake is correctly baked it normally springs back when lightly touched or when a skewer inserted into the centre comes out clean, this is because there is no raw batter left. So when the centre of the cake is cooked it can be confidently taken out of the oven because if the centre is cooked the whole cake is cooked. Further baking beyond that simply drives moisture out of the cake making it dry and with a reduced eating quality and shorter shelf life.

When you bake a cake it's very important to purchase the correct ingredients, weigh them accurately, use the right tin, follow the recipe correctly and bake the cake at the correct temperature. All these actions are obvious and sound simple enough. There is however another aspect that is nearly always overlooked, something my tutors would have called the post baking aspect. When you remove your cake from the oven and hopefully gaze at how beautifully it has turned out it is still possible to ruin your cake, or at least end up with a slightly less than perfect result by what you do next.

During the baking process steam is created by the application of heat to the wet ingredients (eggs, butter, milks or creams). This steam evaporates as the cake bakes and also as the cake cools because the moisture is still escaping. Most people think that the correct procedure is to place your cakes onto a wire rack, now in terms of cooling your cake down quickly that does work, however, it also allows the moisture to escape. If you look at the recipes in this book I only place a cake onto a wire rack to glaze with a syrup or icing which needs to run off the cake. I don't cool cakes on wire racks but usually cover the tins with cloths until they are tepid and rested enough to remove from the tins, I then place them into an airtight box with a lid usually while still tepid and on the base of the tin to prevent possibly breaking it. I know what you are thinking, why would you do that?

Let me explain. if the moisture within the cake is allowed to escape by placing on a wire rack it will be dryer than if you cover them with a cloth before placing into an airtight box. This is because if the moisture cannot evaporate because the cloth is on top of the cake this means the moisture stays within the cake. If you leave your cake on a wire rack the cakes will be dryer in texture particularly on the crust which means your cakes stale quicker because they contain less moisture which not only shortens the shelf life but lessens the eating quality. Cakes should not have a hard crust or be dry to eat they should be soft and delicate. The exception to this is brownie type cakes where a crust is a requirement.

I store all my cakes in airtight containers with tight fitting lids, I use the range made by Stewarts and I buy mine from Nisbets (page 94). If you place a Victoria sandwich in one of these and have the patience to wait 24 hours you will eat a light, beautifully soft cake and wonder why on earth you didn't do this before.

There is another process that needs to be understood, cakes have a different texture 12-24 hours later post baking. This is because the moisture within the cake is trapped within the crumb of the baked product which mellows and releases moisture over time producing a softer crust and a more tender cake crumb after a period of resting.

Another aspect which is particularly true of cakes that contain fruit is that the flavours really come through the day after baking. The lemon cake in this book is one of my favourite recipes but I wouldn't think of eating it within the first 12 hours. After resting for at least 12 hours the crumb mellows and the lemon flavour is really punchy and full.

Several of the recipes need to be stored in the fridge because of the icing or buttercream and where required the recipe says so with the recommendation to bring all refrigerated cakes to room temperature before serving. Most of the cakes can and should be stored at room temperature in an airtight container with a tight fitting lid. Cake tins with loose fitting lids will not keep your cake fresh or for very long. Most cakes in this book will keep for 3-4 days in an airtight box and buttercream cakes for 2-3 days in the fridge.

There is another option and that is to freeze your cakes. All the cakes in this book freeze well if wrapped tightly in a couple of layers of cling film, there are some things to be aware of when freezing the cakes in this book.

Iced cakes like the Diabolo should be wrapped and frozen without icing them, then the cake sponges should be removed from the freezer, defrosted and then iced as per each recipe. This is also true of the Battenberg cake as the marzipan doesn't freeze well.

Buttercream cakes can be frozen with the icing on but if you want to do this the trick is to place the cake uncovered in the freezer and wait until the cake is frozen hard then wrap in cling film and place back into the freezer, this way you won't ruin the icing. Of course you could freeze the sponges not iced then remove from the freezer and finish. I usually place a sheet of parchment paper in between each sponge and wrap all of the sponges together in cling film.

If I could convey one piece of information above everything else in this book it would be how important it is to store your cakes correctly and wait until they peak. So many people have said to me "I know you said wait until the next day but we ate it anyway and it was ok". To me this is like someone drinking a bottle of wine the day you bottle it, good things are worth waiting for and trust me on this 99% of cakes taste better and have a much better texture 12-24 hours later.

Ingredients

Flour

I use Marriages plain flour in my cakes and if this is unavailable Moul Bie T55 is a good swap. If you cannot get hold of either of these then use the best quality plain flour you can find. I don't use self raising flour as the lift is unreliable depending on the age of the flour.

Baking powder & bicarbonate of soda

I personally prefer Dr Oetker baking powder because it's gluten free. Baking powder and bicarbonate of soda off any supermarket shelf is fine just make sure they are fresh and well within shelf life so that they work correctly.

Butter

I only use unsalted and I prefer Country Life or Waitrose own brand.

Chocolate

In this book I use white, milk, dark 55% and 70% varieties. I generally use Callebaut and Cocoa Barry and occasionally some high end single origin chocolate made by Ameidi and Valrhona. As with all chocolates use pure cocoa butter chocolates that do not contain vegetable fats. Most supermarkets or online shops sell good quality chocolate. I prefer to use callets or buttons because they melt easily. If you can only get bars chop these into chunks before melting but be beware of contamination from chopping boards.

Fruits

Wherever possible use fruit in season and perfectly ripe, if you use citrus fruit try and buy unwaxed ones, if you can't find these it's a good idea to wash your citrus fruit in hot water and wipe dry with a tea towel to remove any wax from the skin. I do use frozen blueberries for this book and find them more consistent and better flavour. However, fruits for decoration should always be fresh.

Cocoa powder

Buy the best quality one you can find I use Cocoa Barry extra brut but Green and Blacks organic is very good also.

Dried fruits

I use Whitworths dried fruits particularly mini currants, juicy raisins and sunshine sultanas which are excellent quality. I prefer Morello type glacé cherries over normal ones if you can find them. I buy my candied lemon peel from Keylink but chopped mixed peel is an acceptable substitute if you buy the best quality you can find.

Coconut

I use Whitworth's desiccated coconut which is good quality but a little coarse, I usually blitz mine in a food processor or spice grinder briefly before using.

Polenta

Polenta is used in one recipe in this book, you need to buy the dried ground cornmeal not the prepared wet mixture, I buy mine from online stores or Waitrose.

Jams

I only use Bonne Maman conserves as the flavour is outstanding, they also have a high percentage of fruit to sugar so when they are sieved and reduced they do not become overly sweet when used. See page 74 for instructions on how to prepare conserves or jam for use in this book.

Flavours, Extracts & Colours

I use Nielsen Massey vanilla, almond, coffee and lemon extracts which are excellent quality. More specialist flavours can be bought off the shelf in most supermarkets or from online stores like Sugar Shack. I prefer to use good quality liquid colours or blend my own from very strong powder colours. Use gel colours if you prefer. With all colours and flavours use with discretion as they vary quite a lot in strength and quality.

Nuts

Nuts off the supermarket shelf are fine for the recipes in this book, however, I tend to buy my ground hazelnuts and top grade green pistachios wholesale from online stores.

Glycerine

Glycerine is a humectant meaning it attracts moisture, if you add this to your cakes it extends the shelf life. It is easily available in supermarkets but if you can't find it just miss it out glycerine as it's not vital to the recipe only to the shelf life.

Spices

Dried spices off the shelf of a supermarket are fine for these recipes. I prefer to grind my own cinnamon from sticks as I need them, if possible in a spice grinder. Buy spices as fresh as you can and keep in an airtight container or jar to preserve the aroma and flavour. It's best to purchase these in small quantities to ensure freshness.

Sugars

For the recipes in this book I use caster and granulated white sugar the Tate and Lyle brand. Each of these can be purchased easily in the supermarket. Be careful not to substitute sugars in the recipes, golden caster sugar for instance will generally not work well as a substitute for white caster sugar so use the sugar specified in the recipe.

Syrups & Honey

I use Tate & Lyle golden syrup and clear honey, you don't need anything special for the honey cake but obviously a good quality one will taste better. I like acacia honey in particular.

Alcohol

There are a few recipes in this book where alcohol is used. I buy good quality liquors and use these sparingly, of course if you preference is to not use any alcohol miss them out they are there purely for flavour.

Eggs

All the eggs in this book are medium and net weight of 50g when shelled.

Vanilla

I use fresh vanilla pods in my recipes for this book, these are quite expensive but can be purchased easily via online stores (cheaper than supermarkets). Although the pods are expensive they should be washed then dried and re-used. Second hand vanilla pods can be used again for infusing sauces and ice creams or after several uses dried out and stored in jars of sugar to make lovely vanilla sugar.

Ginger

I use fresh powdered and stem ginger in syrup in my recipes, fresh and powdered are easy to get hold of. For the stem ginger I prefer the Opies brand. I always blend the entire jar, syrup and all into a lovely ginger puree which I place back into the jar then store in the fridge.

Milk & Creams

I use whole milk for my recipes, whipping cream and double cream all easily available off the shelf of any supermarket.

Nut Pastes

I use 50/50 hazelnut praline paste made by Callebaut for my chocolate hazelnut paste other brands are available and easy to purchase online.

Tim Loves

Listed below are websites of suppliers and people I admire and work with.

www.nisbets.co.uk
Pastry equipment, baking trays, cake tins, parchment paper, piping bags and general equipment. I buy nearly all my equipment for my pastry classes from them.

Keylink.org
Pastry ingredients including nuts and chocolate, supplier of pastry bowls and small equipment plus candied fruits.

www.infusions4chefs.co.uk
Specialist pastry ingredients, nuts, chocolate and decor items.

www.chocolateecstasytours.com
My amazing friend Jennifer Earle who is a leading chocolate expert and tour guide who runs chocolate tours around London. Great friend and food expert.

Flour.co.uk
Marriages flour is the only flour I use for my classes because of its quality and consistency.

sugarshack.co.uk
Flavours and extracts, cake cards and ingredients.

Waitrose.com
Flavours, butter, eggs and sugars.

prettysweet.london
Bespoke patisserie by Claire Clarke & Sarah Crouchman.

Lakeland.co.uk
For baking equipment and ingredients.

Pastry Classes

Tim's Pastry Club classes have been running since October 2015 and are full of many wonderful people, many of whom I now call friends. I have people come to classes who have never baked and people who are professional chefs at all levels. My youngest baker was 4 (supervised) and my oldest 74! What I love about the classes is that whatever level people are at, they all have a wonderful time baking, making friends and invariably the students go home with products very similar in quality to the ones I make.

When I set the classes up I wanted to have all the things in the class that I loved at college, with all the negative things removed. This means all the ingredients are weighed up for the students, the equipment is all set out on the table and the recipes are typed out and waiting for them. We also make fresh coffee and proper tea which is always on tap. I always demo the items first and try to explain exactly how and why you do what you do, to get the right results. I spend much of the lessons dispelling myths like you need cold hands to make pastry and explaining why cake batters curdle. All the students go home with typed recipes and a box full of goodies.

All the classes are personally taught by me and can be booked via my website

www.timspastryclub.com

Acknowledgements

No piece of work that requires so much checking and examination could be completed without lots of help and encouragement, many thanks to these amazing people.

Roger White my brilliant web designer at JWS Tech for his technical knowledge, quiet common sense, brilliant ideas and creative enabling, nothing could be done without him.

Jennifer Earle
For writing the lovely forward to this book and always being on hand to answer queries about chocolate.

Jane Johnson
Pastry club student and great friend for recipe testing, proof reading and great advice. A competent baker and foodie who always offers great help and insights.

Jane Day
Brilliant friend who is always energetic, uplifting and encouraging. A talented baker who is always happy to recipe test and willing to help. Her input to my classes and demos has been incredibly helpful.

Martin Llewellyn for recipe testing, creative input and proof reading.

Bella Worland Recipe testing and friendship.

Anne Lee Recipe testing and friendship.

Matt Alner fellow Beatles nut, great friend and recipe tester.

Rhi Haywood Brilliant chef and friend, recipe testing.

Simoney Kyriakou recipe testing, brilliant humour and friendship.

Sarah Pink recipe testing, friendship and great ideas.

Rosie Smith Brilliant chef and friend, recipe testing.

All the lovely ladies at the two Caterham WI groups for friendship and support.

Weights & Measures

No baker or pastry chef from keen amateur to seasoned professional would ever make a cake without using scales. When I started out in the trade a very long time ago we still used pounds and ounces. Nowadays it's universally agreed that grams are much more accurate and small ingredients like raising agents, salt, spices and small liquids like milk are weighed using measuring spoons. I personally dislike spoons and would rather use a micro scale but I am very aware that most people would simply screw their face up at this suggestion as being too finicky. The measurements are set out in simple to follow instructions and I hope very user friendly.

All the dry ingredients like flours and sugars that are larger than spoon sizes are weighed in grams on a digital scale, I use several types of scales but as long as you have one that weighs from 1g to 2kg that will be fine. If you do not have one they are a sound investment and essential for anyone who wants to bake.

All small measures like baking powder, salt, spices, milk and other ingredients like glycerine are measured with spoons so you will need a set. If you do not own a set these are easy to purchase online. For accurate dry measures, scoop the ingredient and tap gently on the container or against the side of a bowl for the contents to settle then run off level with the back of a knife or your finger.

All dry measurements in this book are level spoons and abbreviated as follows

Tsp = Teaspoon in divisions as 1/8, 1/4, 1/2 (for 3/4 tsp use 1/4 & 1/2 tsp)
Tbsp = Tablespoon

Liquid measures are to the top of the spoon.

Measuring Tips

Read each recipe carefully and weigh as the recipe suggests. If the recipe is the creaming method I tend to place the bowl for the stand mixer onto the scale and set to zero then add the butter and set back to zero and add the sugar and flavouring then proceed as laid out in the recipe. Seasoned bakers and cake makers know these things and probably do them without thinking but read the recipe carefully and make sure you weigh up everything accurately and logically.

Most of the recipes call for dry ingredients to be sifted onto parchment paper and set aside. I weigh the flour in a bowl with salt, spices and raising agents into a bowl then sift this onto a separate sheet of parchment paper and place aside so it's ready when I need it.

I use the microwave a lot to melt butter or chocolate I weigh the ingredients on the scale already in the bowl to save time and washing up.

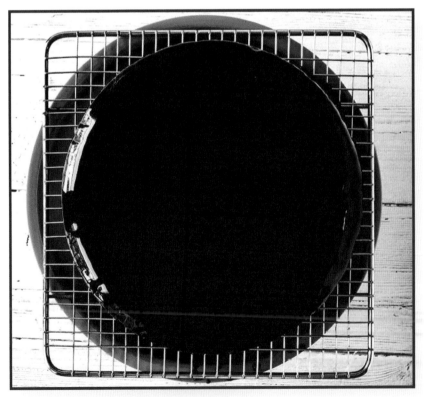

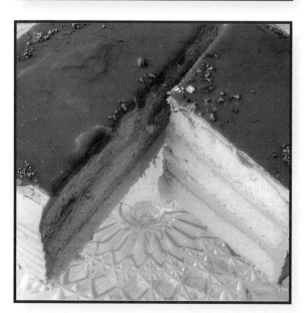

103

Ingredient Index

Ingredient Index

Printed in Poland
by Amazon Fulfillment
Poland Sp. z o.o., Wrocław